Weapons of
Mass Destruction

Other books in the Current Controversies series

Current
CONTROVERSIES

Weapons of Mass Destruction

Michael Logan, Book Editor

GREENHAVEN PRESS

An imprint of Thomson Gale, a part of The Thomson Corporation

THOMSON
™
GALE

Detroit • New York • San Francisco • New Haven, Conn. • Waterville, Maine • London • Munich

THOMSON
GALE

Bonnie Szumski, *Publisher*
Helen Cothran, *Managing Editor*

© 2006 Thomson Gale, a part of The Thomson Corporation.

Thomson and Star logo are trademarks and Gale and Greenhaven Press are registered trademarks used herein under license.

For more information, contact:
Greenhaven Press
27500 Drake Rd.
Farmington Hills, MI 48331-3535
Or you can visit our Internet site at http://www.gale.com

LIBRARY OF CONGRESS CATALOGING-IN-PUBLICATION DATA

Weapons of mass destruction / Michael Logan, book editor.
  p. cm. -- (Current controversies)
Includes bibliographical references and index.
ISBN 0-7377-2785-3 (lib. hardcover : alk. paper) -- ISBN 0-7377-2786-1 (pbk. :
alk. paper)
1. Weapons of mass destruction. 2. National security--United States. 3. Terrorism-
-United States--Prevention. I. Logan, Michael, 1956–
  U793.W426 2007
  358'.3--dc22
                                                          2006020107

Printed in the United States of America
10 9 8 7 6 5 4 3 2 1

Contents

A missile defense system cannot ensure that America will be completely protected from missile-based attacks, nor can it deter terrorists from using weapons of mass destruction within the United States.

Chapter 3: Was Iraq a Weapons of Mass Destruction Threat?

Yes: Iraq Was a Weapons of Mass Destruction Threat

Chapter 4: Can the Proliferation of Weapons of Mass Destruction Be Stopped?

Foreword

By definition, controversies are "discussions of questions in which opposing opinions clash" (*Webster's Twentieth Century Dictionary Unabridged*). Few would deny that controversies are a pervasive part of the human condition and exist on virtually every level of human enterprise. Controversies transpire between individuals and among groups, within nations and between nations. Controversies supply the grist necessary for progress by providing challenges and challengers to the status quo. They also create atmospheres where strife and warfare can flourish. A world without controversies would be a peaceful world; but it also would be, by and large, static and prosaic.

The Series' Purpose

The purpose of the Current Controversies series is to explore many of the social, political, and economic controversies dominating the national and international scenes today. Titles selected for inclusion in the series are highly focused and specific. For example, from the larger category of criminal justice, Current Controversies deals with specific topics such as police brutality, gun control, white collar crime, and others. The debates in Current Controversies also are presented in a useful, timeless fashion. Articles and book excerpts included in each title are selected if they contribute valuable, long-range ideas to the overall debate. And wherever possible, current information is enhanced with historical documents and other relevant materials. Thus, while individual titles are current in focus, every effort is made to ensure that they will not become quickly outdated. Books in the Current Controversies series will remain important resources for librarians, teachers, and students for many years.

In addition to keeping the titles focused and specific, great care is taken in the editorial format of each book in the series. Book introductions and chapter prefaces are offered to provide background material for readers. Chapters are organized around several key questions that are answered with diverse opinions representing all points on the political spectrum. Materials in each chapter include opinions in which authors clearly disagree as well as alternative opinions in which authors may agree on a broader issue but disagree on the possible solutions. In this way, the content of each volume in Current Controversies mirrors the mosaic of opinions encountered in society. Readers will quickly realize that there are many viable answers to these complex issues. By questioning each author's conclusions, students and casual readers can begin to develop the critical thinking skills so important to evaluating opinionated material.

Current Controversies is also ideal for controlled research. Each anthology in the series is composed of primary sources taken from a wide gamut of informational categories including periodicals, newspapers, books, United States and foreign government documents, and the publications of private and public organizations. Readers will find factual support for reports, debates, and research papers covering all areas of important issues. In addition, an annotated table of contents, an index, a book and periodical bibliography, and a list of organizations to contact are included in each book to expedite further research.

Perhaps more than ever before in history, people are confronted with diverse and contradictory information. During the Persian Gulf War, for example, the public was not only treated to minute-to-minute coverage of the war, it was also inundated with critiques of the coverage and countless analyses of the factors motivating U.S. involvement. Being able to sort through the plethora of opinions accompanying today's major issues, and to draw one's own conclusions, can be a complicated and frustrating struggle. It is the editors' hope that Current Controversies will help readers with this struggle.

Introduction

Since the September 11, 2001, terrorist attacks against the United States, President George W. Bush has made curtailing the proliferation of weapons of mass destruction (WMD) a primary part of the U.S. War on Terror. Concerned that terrorist organizations such as al Qaeda—the network that carried out the September 11 attacks—could acquire nuclear, chemical, or biological weapons from rogue nations or the former Soviet republics, the president has declared weapons of mass destruction to be the number one threat to the security of the United States and the world. Cut loose from their Cold War context, where they were mostly discussed abstractly in relation to nuclear deterrence, weapons of mass destruction, President Bush told the world, are not limited to nuclear missiles. Small, briefcase-sized nuclear devices or biological weapons could be manufactured in almost any nation proficient in weapons technology. WMD were suddenly, according to the president, mobile, available, and within the means of those committed to obtaining them.

One of Bush's initial strategies to keep terrorists and rogue nations from acquiring WMD technology was to invade Iraq, a nation whose leader, Saddam Hussein, was strongly anti-Amercian and who allegedly had ties to al Qaeda. The president argued that Saddam was building a WMD program, in spite of assurances to the contrary, and would perhaps covertly supply terrorists with such weapons. Upon launching the U.S.-led invasion in 2003, Bush said his intention was to disarm Iraq's military of weapons of mass destruction that could be used against the United States or its allies or to upset the balance of power in the Middle East. Throughout the confrontation and the succeeding postwar years, U.S. forces have yet to turn up any incontrovertible evidence of an Iraqi WMD program.

The failure of the United States to find WMD in Iraq raises questions about the degree and extent to which the Bush administration should be focusing on countering WMD proliferation. Indeed, global WMD proliferation since the invasion of Iraq has continued. For example, the United States had suspected for some time that North Korea, another of America's antagonists, was enriching the uranium necessary to construct atomic bombs. Eventually, in April 2003, the North Korean government admitted during negotiations with China and the United States that it indeed possessed nuclear weapons. In the following year a multinational surveillance effort uncovered a black market network—run by A.Q. Kahn, the "father" of the Pakistan nuclear bomb—that had sold atomic technology and equipment to countries that included North Korea, Libya, and Iran. The latter, an avowed enemy of Saddam's Iraq, is of particular concern to U.S. analysts. Iran and Iraq had used chemical weapons against one another during their war in the 1980s; U.S. and other world officials have long feared that if either nation acquired WMD, it would not hesitate to use them in further confrontations. In addition to its apprehension over the hostile forces that could use such weapons, the United States also recognizes that the former Soviet Union has stockpiles of weapons-grade, enriched uranium and plutonium that could be used in nuclear warheads. With the collapse of the Soviet regime, international observers warn that these stockpiles are not well protected and might be stolen or sold off to terrorists or rogue nations.

With all these examples of potential or real global proliferation, some critics see the preemptive attack on Iraq as a misguided means of thwarting the spread of WMD. In a September 9, 2004, *Wall Street Journal* editorial, U.S. senator Joseph Biden (a Democrat from Delaware) writes:

This administration's effort to turn military pre-emption from a long-standing option into a one-size-fits-all doctrine says to rogue states that their best insurance policy against regime-change is to acquire WMD as quickly as possible—which is one reason North Korea's nuclear arsenal has apparently increased by 400% under this administration's watch.

According to critics like Biden, the Bush administration's focus on aggressive preemption against WMD coupled with a lack of international negotiation may have led to a calamitous situation with respect to nuclear arsenals and other weapons of mass destruction. By seeking to unify a war on terror with a war on WMD, critics charge, the Bush administration has stretched the capabilities of the U.S. military, now occupying both Afghanistan (al Qaeda's host nation) and Iraq, diminished its leverage in diplomatic negotiation by acting unilaterally, and actually prompted other nations to aggressively pursue WMD technology. A more rational approach, some critics have suggested, is to strengthen existing treaties such as the 1970 Nuclear Non-Proliferation Treaty and the 1997 Chemical Weapons Convention agreement to prevent the spread of WMD.

Others have argued that nuclear proliferation may not be a bad thing. Weapons technology is part of the global economy that has reshaped the world, William Langewiesche notes in the November 2005 edition of the *Atlantic*. He maintains that WMD proliferation cannot be stopped because of the globalization of scientific knowledge and technologies. Given that the dissemination of WMD knowledge cannot be halted, Charles V. Peña, a proliferation analyst, has argued that it is better for all democratic nations to have a WMD arsenal to counter rogue nations who acquire them. Thus, if North Korea has nuclear weapons, it may be in Japan's interest to rethink its ban on nuclear weapons research and development rather than let North Korea destabilize the region. In a 2006 article, Peña wrote, "There was no historical evidence of Iraq, or any other rogue state, using weapons of mass destruction against enemies capable of inflicting unacceptable retaliatory damage.... The belief that all proliferation is equally threatening and dangerous illustrates the problem with the arguments over Iraq's weapons of mass destruction."

Weapons of mass destruction have become tied to United States foreign policy, guaranteeing the debate over WMD will continue for decades to come. In this anthology various authors debate whether weapons of mass destruction are the greatest threat to world security and whether Iraq was ever a WMD threat. The authors also discuss whether the proliferation of weapons of mass destruction can ever be stopped and how the United States can best defend itself from a WMD attack. Such issues will remain of interest as long as WMD proliferation continues to shape the balance of power in the twenty-first century.

CHAPTER 1

Weapons of Mass Destruction: the Most Serious Threat to Global Security?

Chapter Preface

In September 2002, U.S. secretary of defense Donald Rumsfeld told the Senate Armed Services Committee that Iraqi leader Saddam Hussein "has, at this moment, stockpiles of chemical and biological weapons, and is pursuing nuclear weapons. If he demonstrates the capability to deliver them to our shores, the world would be changed." The secretary of defense was making the case for war against Iraq, which would culminate in the March 2003 U.S. invasion of that country.

Prior to the invasion the George W. Bush administration consistently argued that weapons of mass destruction (WMD) in the hands of outlaw nations and leaders like Saddam Hussein posed the greatest threat to humanity. Furthermore, supporters of an invasion of Iraq suggested that if Saddam's WMD programs were not silenced, Iraq may begin disseminating them to other unstable regimes or even terrorist organizations. The Bush administration proposed that the best method to ensure world security was to preemptively disarm Iraq of its alleged weapons and WMD infrastructure. With fears of terrorism and weapons of mass destruction running high in a nation so recently stung by the terrorist destruction of the World Trade Center, the government found enough approval to carry out its plan.

Around the world, though, America did not always find that fear of weapons of mass destruction was a persuasive argument for war. Some world leaders argued that while WMD were certainly a danger they could not be judged in isolation of the myriad problems of humanity. In 2005, Brazilian president Luiz Inacio Lula da Silva told a group of world leaders, "Hunger is the best weapon of mass destruction which exists today. It's killing men, women and innocent children, even before they have a chance to cry and say 'I'm hungry'!" In 2004, United Nations secretary-general Kofi Annan told an audience in Germany:

> In the daily lives of most people in the world today, terrorism and weapons of mass destruction are remote and hypothetical threats. The fears that stalk most people are those of poverty, starvation, unemployment, and deadly disease. When they are threatened with weapons, it [is] most often with those that we might call weapons of individual destruction—Kalashnikovs [automatic rifles], machetes, landmines and the like—in societies where law and order have broken down.

Even in America, Jeffrey Sachs, the influential director of the Earth Institute at Columbia University in New York, wrote for *The Economist*: "If George Bush spent more time and money on mobilizing Weapons of Mass Salvation (WMS) in addition to combating Weapons of Mass Destruction (WMD), we might actually get somewhere in making this planet a safer and more hospitable home." Sachs linked the fight against terrorism to the fight against global poverty: "If Mr. Bush would only lead his country to that end [fighting global poverty and disease] . . . he would mobilize billions of people in the fight against terrorism."

Since the September 11, 2001, terrorist attacks and the subsequent invasions of Afghanistan and Iraq, the United States has organized domestic and foreign policy around the notion that WMD are the world's greatest threat to global security. As a result, the government has restructured its intelligence agencies, formed the Department of Homeland Security, tightened immigration standards, and passed antiterrorist legislation such as the controversial Patriot Act. The question whether the emphasis on WMD and terrorism justifies these changes and the impact they have on Americans and the rest of the world is one that will be asked repeatedly in the years ahead. The authors in the following chapter offer differing viewpoints on the legitimacy of calling WMD the world's greatest threat.

Weapons of Mass Destruction Threaten the United States and Western Democracy

Charles Krauthammer

Charles Krauthammer is a nationally syndicated columnist for the Washington Post Writers Group. He won the 1987 Pulitzer prize for distinguished commentary.

Thank God for Hans Blix. Whenever we become lax and forgetful about how the world changed on Sept. 11, [2001,] former [UN] chief [weapons] inspector Blix is there to make the case for mindless complacency. In a [June 28, 2004,] speech in Vienna [Austria] he warned that one should be wary of the claim that "the risk that reckless groups and governments might acquire weapons of mass destruction is the greatest problem facing our world today." Why? Because "to hundreds of millions of people around the world, the big existential issue is hunger, and also that wherever you live on this planet, the risk of global warming and other environmental threats are existential."

Here we are at the crux of a debate over the United States' aggressive interventionism [since September 11, 2001]. Is Islamic radicalism in potential alliance with terrorist states that possess such weapons a threat to the very existence (hence: "existential") of the United States and of civilization itself?

Forgetting the Lessons of September 11

On Sept. 12, 2001, and for many months after, that proposition was so self-evident that it commanded near unanimous support. With time—[several] years in which, contrary to every expectation and prediction, the second shoe never dropped—that consensus has evaporated.

The new idea, expressed by Blix representing the decadent European left, and . . . amplified by [documentary filmmaker] Michael Moore representing the paranoid American left, is that this existential threat is vastly overblown. Indeed, deliberately overblown by a corrupt/clueless (take your pick) President [George W.] Bush to justify American aggression for reasons of . . . and here is where the left gets a little fuzzy, not quite being able to decide whether American aggression is intended simply to enrich multinational corporations—or maybe just Halliburton alone—with fat war contracts, distract from alleged failure in Afghanistan, satisfy some primal masculine urge or boost poll ratings.

There are no countermeasures to a dozen nuclear warheads detonating simultaneously in U.S. cities.

Ignorance as Entertainment

We have come a long way [since September 11, 2001]. The idea that Sept. 11 was a historic turning point, a wake-up call to a war declared by our enemies but ignored by us, has begun to fade. The week after the attacks, the late-night comedy shows went dark—and upon returning to the air they were almost apologetic about telling jokes, any jokes, ever again. Today, Moore produces a full-length film parody of Sept. 11 and its aftermath [*Fahrenheit 911*] that is not just highly celebrated but commands a huge popular audience. To be sure, Moore's version is not quite as crazed as the French bestseller claiming that the planes that crashed into the World Trade Center were remotely controlled by the CIA at the behest of the president. Moore merely implies some sinister plot, citing connections between the Bush [family] and [the family of al-Qaeda terrorist leader Osama bin Laden]. It's a long way from [2002], when Rep. Cynthia McKinney was run out of Congress for suggesting that Bush had foreknowledge. . . .

Unlike the French book or the Moore movie, Blix is not deranged. He is merely in denial, discounting the uniqueness of the WMD-terrorism issue by comparing it to global warming and hunger. Yes, hunger is an existential issue to the people suffering it. As are car accidents, heart disease and earthquakes. But they hardly threaten to destroy civilization. Hunger is a scourge that has always been with us and that has not been a threat to humanity's existence for at least 1,000 years. Global warming might one day be, but not for decades, or even centuries, and with a gradualness that will leave years for countermeasures.

It is a new world and exceedingly dangerous.

America Is at Stake

There is no gradualness and there are no countermeasures to a dozen nuclear warheads detonating simultaneously in U.S. cities. Think of what just two envelopes of anthrax did to paralyze the capital of the world's greatest superpower. A serious, coordinated attack on the United States using weapons of mass destruction could so shatter America as a functioning, advanced society that it would take generations to rebuild.

What is so dismaying is that such an obvious truth needs repeating. The passage of time, the propaganda of the anti-American left and the setbacks in [the rebuilding of] Iraq have changed nothing of that truth. This is the first time in history that the knowledge of how to make society-destroying weapons has been democratized. Today small radical groups allied with small radical states can do the kind of damage to the world that in the past only a great, strategically located and industrialized power such as Germany or Japan could do.

It is a new world and exceedingly dangerous. Everything is at stake. We are now deeply engaged in a breast-beating exercise for not having connected the dots before Sept. 11. And yet here we are ... years after Sept. 11, with the dots already connected, and we are under a powerful urge to ignore them completely.

Nuclear Terrorism Is a Serious Threat to the United States

Graham Allison

Graham Allison is the director of the Belfer Center for Science and International Affairs at Harvard University. He served as an adviser to the secretary of defense under President Ronald Reagan and assistant secretary of defense under President Bill Clinton. He is the author of Nuclear Terrorism: The Ultimate Preventable Catastrophe.

President [George W.] Bush says the ultimate nightmare for our country is the world's most destructive technologies in the hands of the world's most dangerous actors. What's the world's most destructive technology? Nuclear. Who are the world's most dangerous actors? Terrorists. Senator [John] Kerry, the Democratic challenger [in the 2004 presidential race], said in his June 1 [2004] speech on this topic, "This is the gravest threat to American lives and liberties." He begins to help us think about what would actually happen in our country if such an attack occurred, in a city where it wasn't our city. So it happens in Boston and you're living in San Francisco, or it happens in San Diego. This is really the only existential threat to America as we know it: a free society with the freedoms that we so much value, that plays a leading role in the world. Senator Kerry also says this is the most urgent threat that we face today. If you go across the national security community, of people who have looked at this evidence, there is not a whole lot of disagreement about the gravest threat we're facing.

When the Cold War was over—and we did win—the nuclear weapons themselves didn't go away. And the materials from which nuclear weapons can be made have half-lives of

Graham Allison, "Preventing Nuclear Terrorism," www.commonwealthclub.org, September 20, 2004. Reproduced by permission.

thousands of years; they didn't go away. So we are left with a lot of mess from the Cold War; some of it in more dangerous conditions than even during the Cold War period. As former Secretary of Defense William Perry and former Senator Sam Nunn have said, the chance of a single nuclear bomb exploding in an American city today—a single bomb—is greater today than it was during the high Cold War. The chance of the nuclear Armageddon that we worried about in the Cold War— that is, an attack that would kill everybody in America—is mercifully receded substantially. But the chance of a single nuclear weapon has increased.

Our country has been very successful when it gets itself focused with respect to a problem in addressing it. With respect to this one, we haven't gotten focused.

A Loose Nuke

One month to the day after the 9/11 attacks [staged by the al-Qaeda terrorist organization], George Tenet, as director of central intelligence, walked into the Oval Office to see President Bush to give the president's daily intelligence briefing and informed him that a CIA agent, code-named Dragonfire, reported that a ten-kiloton weapon—that's a small nuclear weapon that would fit in the back of a van—from the former Soviet arsenal was now in control of Al Qaeda and was in New York City. There was a moment of silence, a few deep breaths and then a series of questions. *Could this be happening? Was this a realistic possibility? Did the Soviet arsenal include ten-kiloton weapons?* Yes. *Were all those weapons accounted for?* Uncertain. *Could Al Qaeda have acquired such a weapon?* Yes. *Could Al Qaeda have brought such a weapon to New York City without our knowing about it?* Yes. The U.S. government had no basis in science or in politics to deny or to dismiss this as a real possibility. This is the occasion when Vice President [Richard] Cheney left Washington to stand up an alternative government at a secret location, because there

A ten-kiloton nuclear blast would incinerate everything within a one-third mile radius of ground zero. Library of Congress.

might as well be a nuclear bomb in Washington. And if it went off, the American government might disappear.

In New York City ... you could kill 500,000 people instantly with a nuclear terrorist bomb.

The Nuclear Emergency Search Teams (NEST)—these nuclear ninja specialists—were sent to New York City to look for any traces of a bomb. They didn't tell Mayor [Rudolph] Giuliani, who was somewhat unhappy when he learned about the fact afterwards, but they didn't want to have it leak. . . . Fortunately it turned out to be a false alarm, but it could have happened. There was no basis for dismissing it as a real possibility. And it should help us see, if tomorrow we had another agent who reported that there was another ten-kiloton bomb in San Francisco or Oakland or Boston or Washington, we would have to confront what is a realistic possibility.

How bad would a ten-kiloton bomb be? It would not be the end of the world, it wouldn't be the end of the United States, it wouldn't even be the end of [a major city]. Take ground zero, go out a third of a mile—all that disappears instantaneously. Go out to about a mile and the buildings look like the federal office building in Oklahoma City after Timothy McVeigh, a homegrown American terrorist, bombed it in 1995. In New York City, it depends on the time of day, you could kill 500,000 people instantly with a nuclear terrorist bomb. Just a ten-kiloton bomb, Dragonfire's bomb. Another half a million people might die in a very short order.

If [terrorists] bought a weapon last week, they could have it here [in the United States] now and they could use it tonight.

Four Million Dead

Four million is the answer to the question of [al Qaeda leader] Osama bin Laden's stated objective for America and Americans. His press spokesman, several months after the 9/11 attack, announced on the Al Qaeda web site their objective to kill 4 million Americans, including 2 million children, and to maim an equivalent number. I never understood what this children thing was about, but after the [September 2004] events in Russia at the school [where terrorists held hundreds of schoolchildren and teachers hostage], this came back as a bit of an echo.

How does he get this number? He presents the calculus of what he says is required to balance the scales of justice for the deaths and injuries that what he calls the Jewish/Christian crusaders (by this he means Israel and [the United States]) have caused to Muslims. . . . He adds it up, says it's 4 million. How many 9/11 attacks would it take to kill 4 million Americans? About 1,400. So you are not going to get there by hijacking airplanes and crashing them into buildings.

Inevitable and Preventable

I believe that the analysis leads overwhelmingly to the conclusion that if the U.S. government just keeps doing what it's doing today and what it's been doing for the last several years, and if the other governments of the world just keep doing what they are doing today, a nuclear terrorist attack is inevitable; indeed, I think it's imminent. I make the odds of it more likely than not in the next decade; I don't see any reason why it's not happening already.

Who could do it? Al Qaeda, but also some others. What could they do it with? A nuclear bomb like the ten-kiloton bomb out of the former Soviet arsenal. It's a pre-made bomb but it could come from Russia, from Pakistan, from North Korea perhaps. Or it could be a homemade nuclear bomb (not a dirty bomb) that would have a fission explosion that would make something like this ten-kiloton blast. It would look like Hiroshima [the site of the first atomic bomb explosion in Japan]—and it would be actually made from the Hiroshima design: very robust, simple design. Where would they get it? Russia, most likely. Not because Russia wants to lose any weapons or material, but on the Willie Sutton principle. Remember Willie Sutton, the famous bank robber? He said he robbed banks because that's where the money was. Most of the stuff is in Russia, and lots of it remains, unfortunately. Despite the Nunn-Lugar Cooperative Threat Reduction Program [which helped remove fissile material from the former Soviet Union] and the great work that [former secretary of defense] Bill Perry and [former deputy assistant secretary of defense] Gloria Duffy and other people did on it, about half of that material still remains vulnerable. About half—[since 1991].

When could this happen? If they bought a weapon last week, they could have it here now and they could use it tonight. If they got 100 pounds of highly enriched uranium, which is smaller than a football of material, they could make a bomb in less than a year. How could they get it here? Count the ways. If you have any doubt about a terrorist's ability to bring a nuclear bomb to Boston or San Francisco, they could always hide it in a bale of marijuana.

We have the problem of all the [nuclear] stuff we've already made—which is a lot.

Unlike many forms of terrorism, this ultimate catastrophe is actually preventable. How can this be true?

The strategic marrow of this problem is preventing terrorists from acquiring highly enriched uranium or plutonium. There are only two things known to mankind from which you can make a fission explosion: highly enriched uranium and plutonium. Neither of these occur in nature, so you can't go dig them up. Neither of these can you make in your basement or in your bathtub or laboratory. Making highly enriched uranium or plutonium takes multi-billion dollar investments in a huge industrial facility that takes a number of years to construct and to operate. In principle, one could simply have no more production of such material. A world that decided this was just not going to happen has the ability to watch, to look and even to intervene to prevent additional material being created.

Then we have the problem of all the stuff we've already made—which is a lot. But what do human beings know about locking up things we don't want people to steal? A lot. The United States loses no gold from Fort Knox, not an ounce. Russia loses no treasures from the Kremlin armory, none. So could you imagine locking up all nuclear weapons and all nuclear material as securely as you do gold? I had this argument with somebody in Washington last week. They said, *This is a fantasy. You are going to lock up nuclear weapons as good as gold?* I said, "Why not?" After the first nuclear bomb, people would say it was crazy not to lock up nuclear weapons and materials as good as gold.

The Three No's

I try in part two of [my book] *Nuclear Terrorism* to organize a global campaign to prevent nuclear terrorism under a doctrine of "Three No's." First, no loose nukes. Second, no new nascent nukes. And third, no new nuclear weapons states.

No loose nukes would mean defining with Russia a new gold standard and securing all the weapons and all the materials in the United States and Russia—in the fastest, technically feasible timetable—to this standard in a transparent fashion. Then signing up on a person-by-person basis the leaders of the other nuclear weapons states who would themselves commit to, in their own country, bring all of their weapons and all of their material to this gold standard, in a transparent fashion on the fastest technically feasible timetable.

No new nascent nukes means no new national production of highly enriched uranium and plutonium. Stop now. This brings us to the test case of Iran, which has been rushing down the track and has just come to the last phase in trying to complete its facilities for producing uranium and plutonium. This proposition would go to Iran ... with a global group and offer them a bundle of carrots and an arsenal of sticks by which we would persuade them that their best interests lie in accepting a bargain—what I think of as a grand bargain—for the denuclearization of Iran. There is about an 80 percent chance that ... a focused effort could succeed with respect to Iran, but this window for dealing with Iran is closing. Once they pass the point at which they are actually producing this highly enriched uranium and plutonium, we have a much more difficult problem.

Finally, *no new nuclear weapons states*. There are eight nuclear weapons states. It's not fair that some states have nuclear weapons and others don't; we need to deal with that problem in the longer run, but in any case the problem doesn't get better if there are additional states. Draw a bright line and say, No more. This is challenged . . . by North Korea. Most people don't understand what a dangerous situation this is. Bill Perry has said North Korea is the most dangerous spot on earth. On a 100-point scale, Iraq was a ten and North Korea is a 99, I would say.

What has happened since January of 2003 while we've been consumed by Iraq? North Korea withdrew from the non-proliferation treaty, kicked out the IAEA [International Atomic Energy Agency] inspectors, turned off the video cams that were watching 8,000 fuel rods that have six bombs' worth of plutonium, began trucking these fuel rods off the facilities and has been reprocessing these, and is producing more plutonium. This mysterious explosion that occurred in North Korea fortunately wasn't a nuclear test, but North Korea could conduct a nuclear test and declare itself to be a nuclear weapon state and say that it has an arsenal of a half-dozen weapons and that it's going to complete its production facility for a dozen more a year. If this happens historians will judge it the single greatest failure in American foreign policy ever.

We are racing towards unprecedented catastrophe.

Racing to Catastrophe

I don't actually believe we can live in a world with a nuclear-armed North Korea with a nuclear production. North Korea is an economic basket case. It has three cash crops only. One: missiles, which they sell to anybody who pays. Second: illegal drugs, which they sell whenever they can. And third: counterfeit $100 bills, which they pass out when they can get away with it. So they are looking to have a fourth cash crop, which is nuclear weapons.

I call North Korea "Missiles 'R Us." They sell missiles to whoever wants to buy; they are at risk of becoming "Nukes 'R Us." I believe there is a reasonable chance that we might cause

North Korea to freeze, as the [Bill] Clinton administration did in 1994, and back down this effort on a step-by-step basis, but the window for doing this is very narrow. At some point we may cross the line where this becomes impossible.

At a meeting [in] summer [2004] there was gathered a whole bunch of the national security community, including several former secretaries of defense, former secretaries of state, former national security advisors, former CIA directors—Republicans and Democrats. At the end of the week of talking about nuclear terrorism and what we could do about it, Bill Perry said: *We are racing towards unprecedented catastrophe. I see no sense of urgency in the public. What in the world can we do to awaken the public and energize the administration?* I would say that's the question for all of us.

North Korean Weapons of Mass Destruction Are a Threat To Global Security

Nicholas Eberstadt

Nicholas Eberstadt holds the Henry Wendt Chair in Political Economy at the American Enterprise Institute, a conservative political research institute in Washington, D.C.

Why, exactly, was the declaration by North Korea that it possessed nuclear weapons—and would hold on to its nuclear arsenal "under any circumstances"—greeted with such shock and astonishment around the world?

[North Korean capital] Pyongyang's claim in February [2005] to have joined the world's nuclear weapons club was not exactly a sudden, bizarre and inexplicable whim. Quite the contrary. That announcement represented the entirely logical culmination of decades of steady, deliberate effort and careful, methodical progress on a multifaceted program of weapons of mass destruction (WMD)—including work not only on nuclear weapons, but also chemical and biological weapons and ballistic missiles. To misunderstand this basic truth is to be blind and deaf to the fundamentals of North Korean strategy—an ignorance America and its allies can scarcely afford in the dangerous days that are likely to lie ahead.

When Western commentators have speculated about the motives underlying the North Korean quest for nuclear weapons and other WMD instruments, they have often dwelled upon the theme of "blackmail": that is, the dividends Pyongyang reaps from international military extortion. But this is a highly incomplete explanation of Pyongyang's abiding interests in WMD programs. North Korea's WMD project is aimed

Nicholas Eberstadt, "The Truth About North Korea," *National Interest*, Summer 2005.

at rather more than simply cadging deliveries of food or fuel when the wolf is at the door. Indeed, the purposes of its WMD programs are so closely wedded to purposes of state that they can be described as integrally fused into the very logic of the North Korean system. That strategy, and the logic undergirding it, may be intuitively unfamiliar to those of us with modern, "globalization era" sensibilities. But until we appreciate the thinking that animates North Korea's WMD quest, we will face the prospect of ever more unpleasant and expensive surprises from Pyongyang.

Ready for War

The Democratic People's Republic of Korea (DPRK) [North Korea] is a state unlike any other on the face of the earth today. It is a political construct specially built for three entwined purposes. The first purpose is to fulfill a grand ideological vision: the reunification of the now-divided Korean Peninsula under the unfettered "independent, socialist" rule of the Pyongyang regime—in other words, unconditional annexation of present-day South Korea and liquidation of the government of the Republic of Korea (ROK) [South Korea] so that [North Korean leader] Kim Jong-il and company might exercise total command over the entire Korean race (*minjok* in Korean).

In the view of North Korean leaders, their country is at war today, here and now.

If that sounds preposterous and utterly impracticable to us, understand that things look very different from Pyongyang. North Korean statecraft has been predicated on that very vision for over half a century. To this day, the Sunshine Policy [diplomacy between North and South Korea] and all the rest notwithstanding, Pyongyang grants diplomatic status to only one "government mission" from Seoul: the legation of the so-called National Democratic Front of South Korea (*Hanminjon*), an invented resistance group supposedly based in the South that regularly uses North Korean airwaves to denounce the Republic of Korea as an illegitimate colonial police state.

The second purpose is to settle a historical grievance, namely the failure of the famous June 1950 surprise attack against South Korea—an assault that might well have unified all of Korea on Pyongyang's terms but for America's unexpected military intervention in defense of the ROK. In Pyongyang's telling, it is only American imperialism that has permitted an otherwise rotten, unstable and irredeemable ROK government to survive since 1950. The total-mobilization war state that Pyongyang has painfully erected over the decades (at the cost of, [among other things] the North Korean famine of the 1990s) is a response to this grievance and an instrument for fulfilling this vision.

To deter ... the United States, [North Korea] must possess nuclear weaponry ... [and be] capable of delivering them into the heart of the American enemy.

The third purpose is to conduct a war, and that war is not some future theoretical contingency. Rather, in the view of North Korean leaders, their country is at war today, here and now. This may help to explain why the DPRK, with its population of more than twenty million, has for years fielded an army of a million-plus soldiers, a military force that currently ranks as the world's fourth largest—larger even than Russia's. Although we are sometimes inattentive to it, the historical fact is that the Korean War's battles were only halted through a cease-fire agreement, the Armistice of 1953. There has never been a peace treaty bringing the hostilities to a formal and conclusive end. The Korean War is, from the DPRK's standpoint, an ongoing war—and North Korea's leadership is committed to an eventual, unconditional victory in that war, however long that may take and however much that may cost.

Nuking America and Asia

Against all odds, the North Korean leadership still attempts to support a vast conventional military force—long rehearsed for an anticipated reprise of June 1950—on a dysfunctional and failing Soviet-style economy. Despite the ingenuity and bravery of the soldiers of the North Korean People's Army (KPA), this conventional force cannot hope to prevail over the combined U.S.-South Korean alliance that awaits them on the other side of the DMZ [demilitarized zone along the North-South border]. America's fearsome firepower—resources that could be trained on North Korea from land, air, sea and space—are by themselves adequate to guarantee not only the annihilation of the KPA, but the complete undoing of the North Korean regime. Thus, the neutralization and effective removal of the United States and the U.S. alliance system from the Korean equation remains utterly essential from Pyongyang's perspective.

That objective, however, cannot be achieved by the DPRK's conventional capabilities, today or in the foreseeable future. To deter, coerce and punish the United States, the DPRK must possess nuclear weaponry and the ballistic missiles capable of delivering them into the heart of the American enemy. This central strategic fact explains why North Korea has been assiduously pursuing its nuclear development and missile development programs for over thirty years—at terrible expense to its people's livelihood, and despite all adverse repercussions on its international relations.

Although Pyongyang rails against "globalization" in other contexts, North Korea's own conception of the uses of WMD are fully "globalized." Thanks largely (though not exclusively) to its short-range SCUD-style missiles and biochemical weapons, primarily targeted on South Korea, Pyongyang can always remind counterparts in the Blue House (South Korea's presidential residence) that the enormous metropolis of Seoul is a hostage to fate, to be destroyed in a moment on Kim Jong-il's say-so. Intermediate No Dong-type missiles capable of striking Japan (and American bases there) with nuclear warheads put Japanese political leaders permanently on alert to the possible costs of incurring North Korea's anger and the potential dangers of siding with the United States in a peninsular crisis. Finally, long-range missiles of the improved Taepo Dong variety may be capable of striking the U.S. mainland, now or in the relatively near future.

Escalating international tensions are not accidental . . . side-effects of [North Korea's WMD] program. They are its central purpose.

There is no indication, incidentally, that North Korean decision-makers view WMD as "special weapons" to be held in reserve. On the contrary, missiles and nuclear devices seem to figure integrally in North Korean official thinking and are *already* being used on a regular basis in North Korean statecraft, as the government's ongoing forays in "blackmail diplomacy" attest. Moreover, despite North Korea's emphasis on race doctrine, there is no indication whatsoever that North Korean leadership would hesitate to use such weapons on *minjok* in South Korea. Pyongyang did not blink at starving perhaps one million of its *own* people for reasons of state in the 1990s. It regards the South Korean state as a cancerous monstrosity, and those who support it as corrupt and worthless national traitors.

WMD Blackmail

Several important implications flow from the DPRK's conception of and strategy for its WMD program. First, continuing and escalating international tensions are not accidental and unwelcome side-effects of the program. They are its central purpose. Simply stated, the DPRK's growing WMD arsenal, and the threats that arsenal permits the North Korean regime to pose to other governments, are the key to the political and economic prizes Pyongyang intends to extract from an otherwise hostile and unwilling world.

Second, WMD threats—especially nuclear and missile threats—have already been used by North Korea with great success as an instrument for extracting *de facto* international extortion payments from the United States and its allies, and as a lever forcing the United States to "engage" Pyongyang diplomatically and on Pyongyang's own terms.

Despite the North Korean regime's seemingly freakish face to the world, the leadership's ability to make subtle and skillful calculations is underscored by the bottom line in its negotiations with the U.S. government [since 1995]. Between 1995 and 2004, according to calculations of the Congressional Research Service, Pyongyang secured more than $1 billion in foreign aid from the United States—a state the DPRK regards as its prime international enemy.

The greatest potential dividends for North Korean nuclear and ballistic diplomacy, however, still lie in store—and this brings us to a third point. For half a century and more, U.S. security policy has been charged with imposing "deterrence" upon Pyongyang. Shouldn't we expect that Pyongyang has also been thinking about how to "deter" the United States over those same long decades?

Breaking the U.S.-South Korea Alliance

Nuclear weapons (especially long-range nuclear missiles) might well answer the "deterrence question" for the North Korean state, as former Secretary of Defense William J. Perry incisively recognized in his 1999 "Perry Process" report. Faced with the risk of nuclear attack on the U.S. mainland, he warned, Washington might hesitate at a time of crisis in the

Korean Peninsula. But if Washington's security commitment to South Korea were not credible in a crisis, the military alliance would be hollow and vulnerable to collapse under the weight of its own internal contradictions. North Korea's WMD program, in short, may be the regime's best hope for achieving its long-cherished objectives of breaking the U.S.-South Korean military alliance and forcing American troops out of the Korean Peninsula.

Fourth, those who hope for a "win-win" solution to the North Korean nuclear impasse must recognize the plain fact that Pyongyang does not now engage in win-win bargaining, and never has. The historical record is completely clear: Pyongyang believes in zero-sum solutions, preferring outcomes that entail not only DPRK victories, but also face-losing setbacks for its opponents. From the DPRK's perspective, win-win solutions are not only impractical (because they leave adversaries unnecessarily strong), but actually immoral as well.

A genuine agreement to denuclearize might well undermine the authority and legitimacy of the North Korean state.

Finally, those who believe that a peaceful and voluntary denuclearization of the DPRK is still possible through further rounds of international conference diplomacy or through some future negotiating breakthrough must be ready to consider how such an outcome would look from North Korea today—that is to say, from the standpoint of the real, existing North Korean state, not some imaginary DPRK we would rather be talking to.

No matter how large the pay-off package, no matter how broad and comprehensive the attendant international formula for recognition and security, the Western desideratum of "complete verifiable irreversible denuclearization" would irrevocably consign North Korea to a world in which the metrics of peaceful international competition matter most—and thus irrevocably to an international role for the DPRK more in consonance with the size of its gross national product. No North Korean leader is likely to regard such a proposal as any bargain.

WMD Trumps Diplomacy

Even worse from Pyongyang's standpoint is that a genuine agreement to denuclearize might well undermine the authority and legitimacy of the North Korean state. Since its founding in 1948, the DPRK has demanded terrible and continuing sacrifices from its population, but it has always justified these in the name of its historic vision for reunifying the Korean race. Today, however, forswearing its WMD options would be tantamount to forswearing the claim to unify the Korean Peninsula on Pyongyang's own terms. Shorn of its legitimating vision, what would be the rationale for absolutist North Korean rule?

The unsettling thrust of this analysis is not just that the North Korean leadership today may positively prefer a strategy that augments the government's WMD capabilities. It may also positively fear a strategy that does anything less. Kim Jong-il is doing his best to make the world safe *for* the DPRK. Our task, by contrast, is to make the world safe *from* the DPRK. This will be a difficult, expensive and dangerous undertaking. For America and its allies, however, the costs and dangers of failure will be incalculably higher.

Al Qaeda Is Likely to Use Weapons of Mass Destruction

Robert Wesley

Robert Wesley is a terrorism analyst specializing in Islamic military trends and weapons of mass destruction.

With the loss of its Afghan sanctuary following the U.S. intervention in 2001, there was a question as to what role weapons of mass destruction (WMD) would play in [terror network] al-Qaeda's newly evolving strategy. Al-Qaeda has taken advantage of its recently assumed role as the ideological and strategic brain for the global jihad [Muslim holy war against infidels] to create an environment from which a variety of jihadi [holy warrior] elements can participate in acquiring and employing chemical, biological, radiological, and nuclear (CBRN) weapons.

Al-Qaeda has opened the door for its supporters to use CBRN weapons to further the goals of the global jihad. To this end, al-Qaeda has provided the religious, practical, and strategic justifications to engage in CBRN activities. These steps have served to strengthen the acceptance of such weapons within sympathetic audiences, dispelled objections to unconventional attacks and prepared the ground for jihadi leaders to operationalize CBRN weapons into their repertoire of tactics. Departing from its previous reliance on in-house production and management of CBRN weapons, al-Qaeda is now encouraging other groups to acquire and use CBRN weapons with or without its direct assistance.

Robert Wesley, "Al-Qaeda's WMD Strategy After the U.S. Intervention in Afghanistan," *Terrorism Monitor*, vol. 3, October 21, 2005. Copyright © 2004. Reproduced by permission.

A Religious Duty to Use WMD

Over the years, al-Qaeda has stepped up its efforts to seek justifications to conduct increasingly brutal attacks. Correspondingly, the group has attempted to frame the acquisition and use of CBRN weapons as the religious duty of Muslims. Al-Qaeda began the process of incorporating this dynamic before the U.S. intervention in Afghanistan. In response to the testing of Pakistan's nuclear arsenal in 1998, [al-Qaeda's leader] Osama bin Ladin praised the efforts of the first Muslim state to defend itself through WMD and encouraged other Muslims to follow Pakistan's example. Shortly after these developments, bin Ladin was interviewed by [TV correspondent for the Arab network, Al-Jazeera] Jamal Isma'il in December of 1998 over U.S. charges that al-Qaeda was aggressively pursuing CBRN. Bin Ladin asserted that using the word "charge" was misleading in that it implies a wrong doing. Rather, according to bin Ladin, "it is the *duty* of Muslims to possess them [WMD]," and that "the United States knows that with the help of Almighty Allah the Muslims today possess these weapons".

Al-Qaeda's pre-9/11 [2001] activities also display a sense of confidence in its preparation to use CBRN weapons.

These events illustrate al-Qaeda's early gravitation toward promoting CBRN weapons that the network was attempting to produce before the U.S. intervention in Afghanistan. Al-Qaeda's pre-9/11 [2001] activities also display a sense of confidence in its preparation to use CBRN weapons. However, in response to the 9/11 attacks, the terror network came under increasing criticism from its Muslim audiences to more correctly follow Islamic traditions of warning, offers of conversion, and significant religious authorization before committing such highly destructive attacks in the future.

Through a series of subsequent statements, al-Qaeda is believed to have sufficiently fulfilled these prerequisite obligations for high-impact attacks. The lesson of 9/11 has also been applied to its WMD strategy, in that further preparations have been taken to justify CBRN attacks prior to the actual events. Al-Qaeda seems to frame its argument around references from the Qur'an [the Muslim holy book] that they interpret as instructing Muslims to respond to aggression with equal aggression (Qur'an 16:126; 2:194; 42:40); similar to the [biblical] expression of "an eye for an eye."

Annihilate All the Infidels

In this regard, Osama bin Ladin stated in 2001 that, "if America used chemical and nuclear weapons against us, then we may retort with chemical and nuclear weapons. We have the weapons as a deterrent". Al-Qaeda also received much needed outside theological assistance from the radical Saudi shaykh Nassir bin Hamad al-Fahd. In 2003, al-Fahd issued an important and detailed fatwa [legal ruling by an Islamic authority] on the permissibility of WMD in jihad. He stated that since America had destroyed countless lands and killed about 10 million Muslims, it would obviously be permitted to respond in-kind. Al-Fahd's ruling provided support to the previous assertion of al-Qaeda spokesman Suleiman Abu Gheith in 2002, stating that, "we have the right to kill 4 million Americans, 2 million of them children . . . and cripple them in the hundreds of thousands. Furthermore, it is our obligation to fight them with chemical and biological weapons, to afflict them with the fatal woes that have afflicted Muslims because of their chemical and biological weapons".

However, these do not constitute the most direct threats of WMD deployment by the terror network. In fact, purported al-Qaeda trainer Abu Muhammad al-Ablaj continued the preparation for eventual WMD use when he forebodingly said in 2003 that, "as to the use of Sarin [nerve] gas and nuclear [weapons], we will talk about them then, and the infidels will know what harms them. They spared no effort in their war on us in Afghanistan and left no weapon but used it. They should not therefore rule out the possibility that we will present them with our capabilities". Al-Ablaj again emphasized the thematic justification of reciprocity concerning WMD. Later in 2003 al-Ablaj provided further explanation that a chemical, biological, or nuclear weapon is a strategic weapon that has "reactions commiserate with its size." He added, "It must therefore be used at a time that makes the crusader enemy beg on his knee that he does not want more strikes". Apparently al-Ablaj is convinced that al-Qaeda has fulfilled its preparatory duty for using CBRN and it is now only a matter of appropriate circumstances presenting themselves.

Although the core of al-Qaeda has been primarily concerned with justifying WMD attacks based on reciprocity, Mustafa Setmariam Nasar (a.k.a. Abu Mus'ab al-Suri), a highly experienced jihadi, veteran of the Afghan conflicts and associate of al-Qaeda and the Taliban [the former Islamic government of Afghanistan], has taken another line of justification. Al-Suri's position is similar to the legal judgment of al-Fahd when he wrote that "if those engaged in jihad establish that the evil of the infidels can be repelled only by attacking them with weapons of mass destruction, they may be used even if they annihilate all the infidels".

WMD Mujahideen

Mustafa Setmariam Nasar was forced out of Afghanistan after the U.S. intervention at the end of 2001. He then devoted the next several years to, as he explains, "plug one of the Muslims' major gaps: reflection on past experience . . . and comparing it with the confrontation and battles which the future holds for us, as I am one of the few mujahideen [Muslim warriors engaged in jihad] remaining who specialized in this matter". The fruit of al-Suri's contemplative hiatus is an unprecedented 1600 page treatise of strategic and military guidance which should be taken very seriously in terms of its impact on the future strategy of the global jihad. He has concluded that CBRN weapons are the "difficult yet vital" means to ensure final victory, partially due to ineffectiveness of current tactics. He also stated that "the mujahideen must obtain them [WMD] with the help of those who possess them either buying them," or by "producing primitive atomic bombs, which are called dirty bombs [RDD]". His prescription of WMD will serve to strengthen the direction of the global jihad towards using CBRN in the future as he has essentially bound the aforementioned broad strategic parameters created by al-Qaeda's traditional leadership into a more actionable logic. Al-Suri, in a sense, has departed from the current strategy of al-Qaeda's traditional leadership. Al-Qaeda's leadership has been primarily concerned with providing the justification for jihadis to use WMD, while al-Suri advances this to actively advocating CBRN weapons as essential to the "end-game" strategy.

It must be recognized that although what has constituted "al-Qaeda" as an organization or network is now undergoing considerable realignment into more of a guidance and support base, it still retains operational capabilities which will be demonstrated in the future. Figures such as Abu Khabab, a director of al-Qaeda's chemical and biological weapons programs believed to be at large, or other members of the former weapons programs, may play a significant role in any future attack. Abdullah al-Muhajir, previously Jose Padilla, is an example of al-Qaeda's traditional cadres' continued intention to plan and execute such attacks. Padilla is accused of meeting with "senior al-Qaeda operatives" while in Pakistan and Afghanistan in 2001 and 2002, who instructed him to return to the United Sates to explore advanced plans for attacking America, including an attack with a radiological weapon (RDD). Lastly, it is also worth noting that the rising class of "e-mujahideen," who are increasingly integrated into the Internet yet have little connection to established jihadi groups, have displayed enthusiasm for WMD.

There are several "encyclopedias" online claiming to contain formulas for chemical agents or construction plans for dirty bombs. Although much of the information provided in these manuals is usually flawed from a technical perspective, the fact that e-mujahideen are promoting WMD procurement and use while disseminating CBRN manuals is quite alarming. It is only a matter of time before more accurate manuals will begin to surface, an eventuality that will make countering CBRN terrorism increasingly more difficult.

CBRN weapons are likely to be employed by jihadi forces in the not-so-distant future.

Only a Matter of Time

Al-Qaeda's leadership has made a concerted effort to prepare its audiences for a WMD attack. However, it has been argued that since the historical volume of direct references to WMD by al-Qaeda has been relatively low, this somehow displays a disinterest in or unlikelihood of WMD playing a role in the terror network's future. Al-Qaeda operative Muhammad al-Ablaj has already responded to this argument when he asked: "Is there a sane person who discloses his [WMD] secrets?" A second explanation is that what has already been presented has adequately justified WMD use, and thus there is little more to be said until a need for further guidance presents itself, such as it did for al-Suri. Whether by al-Qaeda core cadres, those answering al-Suri's calls, or e-mujahideen inspired by their own arguments and supported by al-Qaeda's justifications, CBRN weapons are likely to be employed by jihadi forces in the not-so-distant future.

Small Arms Are a Greater Global Threat than Weapons of Mass Destruction

Raenette Taljaard

Raenette Taljaard is a member of the South African Parliament. She wrote the following article in 2003 as a Yale World Fellow at Yale University.

As the world watched the principal US investigator, David Kay, come up empty-handed in his search for weapons of mass destruction (WMD) in Iraq [in 2003], coalition force soldiers and civilians continued to perish. They are being killed by small arms and light weapons. Rocket-propelled grenades continue to rock the frontline of the post-conflict reconstruction effort as weapons inspectors keep up the hunt for WMD in Iraq. Meanwhile soldiers uncover small arms and light weapons caches with a near hum-drum regularity in Iraq.

The real weapons of mass destruction are not the ones being sought by David Kay in Iraq. To millions of people across the world they are the small arms and light weapons that wreak havoc and cause significant loss of life every day. As UN Secretary-General Kofi Annan has said: "The death toll from small arms dwarfs that of all other weapons systems— and in most years greatly exceeds the toll of the atomic bombs that devastated Hiroshima and Nagasaki [during World War II]. In terms of the carnage they cause, small arms, indeed, could be described as 'weapons of mass destruction.' Yet there is still no global non-proliferation regime to limit their spread."

Calculating Small Arms Destruction

Over 5,000 people died in 1988 in the town of Halabja when the [Saddam] Hussein regime launched a chemical attack on innocent Kurdish Iraqis. This compares with over 300,000 small arms-related deaths per year with incalculable costs for peace and development foregone in some of the most poverty-stricken countries. It is estimated that wars fought with small arms and light weapons in Africa [since 1993] have claimed more than 20 million victims. An estimated 2 million children have been killed, 5 million people have been handicapped, 12 million people have been left without shelter, and 17 million have been driven from their homes and/or countries.

In the same minute in which one person dies from armed violence, 15 new arms are manufactured for sale.

With the global security and disarmament community renewing its focus on the proliferation of WMD in the context of the war on terror, and with new threats to global peace and security emanating from North Korea and Iran, there is a grave danger that the global diffusion of small arms and light weapons will slip onto the backburner of disarmament debates and action.

A recent report by Oxfam and Amnesty International expresses concern that the global campaign against terrorism has made handguns and other small arms more easily available in some countries as suppliers have loosened export controls for states allied to the US in the 'war on terror'. In the same minute in which one person dies from armed violence, 15 new arms are manufactured for sale. There is no doubt that an expansion of the arms caches already in existence today will have dire consequences for developed and developing countries alike.

While WMD is, yet again, taking center-stage, WIDs [weapons of individual destruction] pose an equally grave and great challenge, not only to developing countries gripped in conflict or making their way painstakingly towards demobilization and peace, but to global security. Small arms are tools imminently suitable to exacerbating the phenomenon of failed states. In Africa, small arms also find their way far too easily into the hands of child soldiers, many of whom, orphaned by the ravages of the HIV/AIDS crisis, turn to rebel groups and militias for their livelihood and survival.

A rash of weekly shootings and a [2003] blast that killed an innocent schoolteacher in eastern Kosovo [in Serbia] raised international concern over uncontrolled weapons in this post-conflict zone. With UN estimates putting the number of small arms in Kosovo (ranging from Kalashnikovs to AK47s and rocket propelled grenade launchers) at approximately half a million, the UNDP [United Nations Development Program] recently launched a three month public awareness campaign that will be followed by tough criminal penalties for illegal gun ownership. According to UN estimates, Afghanistan is home to between 500,000 and 1.5 million weapons. Estimates show some 300,000 child soldiers around the world are carrying pistols and machine guns. There are at least 639 million firearms in circulation in the world today, with 1,134 companies in 98 countries actively producing these weapons.

The peddling of small arms and light weapons is deeply embedded in conflict economies.

Producing Human Devastation

There can be no doubt that the spread of WIDs in Africa have exacerbated near-intractable interstate conflicts and civil wars, contributed to human rights violations where the population gets caught in the crossfire, and undermined political and economic development by entrenching conflict economies fuelled by commodities and guns. In sub-Saharan Africa alone it is estimated that 30 million small arms and light weapons are in circulation. Many of these weapons circulate from conflict zone to conflict zone with ruthless arms brokers extracting huge profits. The peddling of small arms and light weapons is deeply embedded in conflict economies—whether civil war–based conflict or conflict intertwined with organized crime syndicates—where natural resources, such as timber, minerals or conflict diamonds or other products such as narcotics are traded for these WIDs. Small arms therefore not only pose a disarmament challenge but also a formidable challenge for development and humanitarian intervention and assistance.

Against this stark backdrop of human devastation, the international community cannot afford to pick favorites for disarmament debates when it has such clear proof that WMD proliferation has caused less loss of human life than WID diffusion across our global village. Worse still, it cannot afford to squander what little political will can and must be mustered to tackle the small arms challenge. Already the signals on political will are disconcerting. The UN Security Council's Expert Panel reports on Sierra Leone, Liberia and Angola reveal how contemptuously arms brokers have defied UN arms embargos and show a near complete inaction on the part of the international community to enforce them. In addition the [2001] UN conference on small arms failed to enact the new small arms non-proliferation regime called for by Secretary General Annan.

The international community must realize the link between small arms and new security threats.

The international community should adopt an all-encompassing new Arms Trade Treaty with clear provisions regulating transfers, marking and tracing of weapons, the role of brokers and containing prohibitions on transfers to non-state actors. Instead, it has failed to rise to the challenge and adopted a mere political agreement—the Programme of Action to Prevent, Combat and Eradicate the Illicit Trade in Small Arms and Light Weapons in All Its Aspects. While the programme of action calls on states to undertake a host of steps at a national, regional and multilateral level, these steps are not binding or compulsory. States can proceed in a discretionary fashion at any pace, if at all.

Linking WID and Security Threats

The failure to commit seriously to addressing the proliferation of WID is unconscionable. The international community must realize the link between small arms and new security threats, and act swiftly to tighten regulatory mechanisms to counteract their proliferation. There can be no more lost opportunities or neglect of WID in favor of WMD disarmament issues. In the post–Cold War security threat world, both WMD and WID must be seen—against the backdrop of failed states—as indispensable parts of a disarmament continuum. This means that key countries, such as the United States, must be willing to engage the crucial questions of the need to establish and maintain controls over private ownership of these deadly weapons and their proliferation to non-state groups. This will require Washington to work hand-in-hand with the international community on disarmament matters.

American Aggression Is a Greater Global Threat than Weapons of Mass Destruction

Mike Whitney

Mike Whitney is a columnist for Counterpunch, *an online political newsletter, as well as a frequent opinion-editorial writer for other Web-based publications.*

Conventional wisdom informs us that "weapons of mass murder" in the hands of terrorists is the greatest danger facing the world today. Regrettably, people from both sides of the political aisle accept this pronouncement as though it was a fundamental law of physics. Leftists are just as apt to advocate ratcheting up surveillance, increasing covert operations and circumventing the law to make sure that, as [President George W.] Bush says, "the world's most dangerous weapons don't get into the hands of the world's most dangerous people."

This could be a mistake. At the very least we should challenge the perceived wisdom and analyze its meaning according to the same principles of justice and security we would apply elsewhere. There's no doubt that the highest ranking members of the Bush administration have thoroughly examined the issue of WMD [weapons of mass destruction]. They have consistently isolated WMD as "the greatest threat facing civilization today." That may be, but the more likely explanation is that WMD is the most serious obstacle facing the Bush administration's skewed plan for world domination.

To begin with, these weapons are always developed by governments who claim that they are vital to insuring the nations' defense. By that logic, who would deny the Palestin-

Mike Whitney, "Rethinking WMD: Deterring the Empire," *Al-Jazeerah.Info*, October 7, 2004. Reproduced by permission.

ians the means to defend themselves against the brutish assault of invaders who are now rampaging through their cities destroying anything and anyone who doesn't fit into Israel's security blueprint?

Who would deny the people of Samarra [the ancient name for Iraq] the means to defend themselves against a carefully calculated massacre by an occupying army trying to establish military rule over a civilian population?

Justice Precedes Safety

By any standard, native people should be provided with the wherewithal to deter aggression. If anything, this suggests more widespread use of WMD. Is this a solution that American liberals would advocate? Of course not. Instead, they have cast their lot with the religious leaders, pacifists and "hand-wringers" of every stripe who have joined Bush's campaign to rid the world of WMD.

The [Bush] administration is telegraphing to the world that WMD is the only real deterrent to their global onslaught.

This is nonsense. Justice must precede safety, and the right to self defense must precede anxiety over bloodier conflicts. The alternative is what we see taking place right now in both Iraq and Palestine. Given half a chance the superior powers have crushed the opposition, stealing land and resources and leaving them in a state of helpless subjugation. How well this matches up with [British novelist] George Orwell's grim prediction for mankind: "If you want a vision of the future, imagine a boot stamping on a human face—forever."

If Iran had WMD in the form of ballistic missiles, you can bet that the spirit of negotiation would be sweeping through [Israel's capital] Tel Aviv and Washington [D.C.] right now. Similarly, if [Iraqi leader] Saddam [Hussein] had nuclear weapons, the administration never would have embarked on their murderous campaign. We shouldn't ignore the implications of these observations. The administration is telegraphing to the world that WMD is the only real deterrent to their global onslaught. There's nothing we can do to change this fact. When public sentiment, democratic institutions and international condemnation fail; what's left is force or the threat of force. Ignoring this dismal reality invites the brutality we are now seeing on a daily basis in Palestine and Iraq.

Aggression Has Replaced Liberation

To a large extent, the war in Iraq has clarified this issue. The Bush team has abandoned the discretion that was the hallmark of previous administrations. Iraq was a candid display of unprovoked aggression. The intention was to send the world a message that the empire would henceforth be governed by an iron fist. To that end, Iraq's wealth has been divided up among Bush supporters and cronies with scant attention to the watchful eyes of the world. Prisoners have been locked away and tortured without the slightest regard for conventions, treaties or international law. As the situation has steadily deteriorated, all pretense of "liberation" or "democratization" has been shorn and replaced with raw military might. The "pacification" of Samarra and Faluja [Iraqi cities] (with their attendant massacres) suggests that the war has entered a new phase that eschews all political solutions, opting instead for West Bank–style [Israeli military occupation] repression. If this is the paradigm of "world order" we are being offered, we need to revisit our conclusions about WMD.

The real question is whether the US monopoly on force is making the world safer.

Is there really no greater threat to humanity than weapons in the hands of the wrong people? Is it a greater threat than

50 or 100 years of Iraq-type interventions to secure the world's resources and subdue the indigenous populations? Is it a greater threat than the *1984* [George Orwell's dystopian novel] world of surveillance and circumscribed liberties that is being constructed for us brick-by-brick by the Bush team?

The Need for WMD

Is it a greater threat than a system that institutionalises torture, war and deception to keep wealth and power in the hands of the few? Most people would like to see a serious reduction, if not a total elimination of WMD. However, this "wishful thinking" does nothing to help us wrestle with the current dilemma. The real question is whether the US monopoly on force is making the world safer and more democratic or tilting the world inexorably towards tyranny. Again, we only need to observe Iraq to make our judgment.

There's no question that WMD will fall into the hands of terrorists, guerillas, insurgents, nationalists, liberation fighters or non-state actors. Their urgent need for such weapons will undoubtedly hasten their success in acquiring them. The question is whether that will signal the end of the "client-based" colonial system that currently reigns supreme or drive the species closer to extinction.

Terrorists Are Not Likely to Use Weapons of Mass Destruction

Shawn Choy

Shawn Choy is a research analyst for the Center for Defense Information, a nongovernmental research organization that monitors military power and international security.

The notion that [the] September [2001] attacks changed everything—that Americans now face a more hazardous geopolitical setting—is by now tired cliché. But rather than changing the actual landscape of threats, the attackers merely unraveled blithe American assumptions regarding terrorist objectives and the means they are willing to employ. Most significantly, the spotlight has since fallen on terrorism involving weapons of mass destruction (WMD).

Nuclear weapons . . . require fissile material in quantities that are beyond the reach of terrorists.

Since . . . September [2001], the mantra of policymakers and the media on WMD terror has been "not if, but when." Never mind the inherent difficulties associated with deploying chemical, biological, and nuclear weapons. Never mind that the four most recent instances of catastrophic terrorism against the United States—the abortive 1993 bombing of the World Trade Center, the 1995 Oklahoma City bombing, and the attacks of September 2001—were perpetrated using conventional high explosives. In a climate of fear, paranoia can easily run afoul of rational judgment.

The Challenge of Using WMD

Not that anyone disputes that [terror] organizations like al Qaeda would perpetrate a WMD attack if they could swing it. The attacks on the World Trade Center and the Pentagon dealt a finishing blow to the conventional wisdom that terrorists value publicity over mass casualties. With the rise of religious extremists, death and destruction have become ends in themselves. Moreover, if these ultraterrorists are willing to forfeit their own lives to maximize results, all previously perceived limits on their intentions are now irrelevant. Intent does not, however, translate directly to threat; intent must be discounted by its improbability, as dictated by terrorists' capabilities. While some might argue that prevention of WMD contingencies should err on the side of caution, such preparations take a toll on measures that address other types of threats. The costs of measures against WMD terrorism should not exceed the degree to which they actually avert terrorism.

In reality, weapons of mass destruction present considerable challenges to anyone trying to procure them without state support. Nuclear weapons, which are the only type of WMD that can cause death on the scale of the September 2001 attacks, require fissile material in quantities that are beyond the reach of terrorists seeking to produce them from scratch. That leaves biological and chemical possibilities, whose manufacture and delivery demand technical savvy, abundant resources, and specialized facilities that non-state groups are not likely to possess.

Japanese doomsday cult Aum Shinrikyo demonstrated these challenges as the only non-state group to successfully launch a large-scale WMD attack on civilians. Despite enjoying atypical advantages over other terrorist groups—an estimated $1.4 billion in assets, an educated staff of over 80 scientists, and modern research facilities—technological obstacles thwarted all but one of their attempts at mass terrorism. And although their 1995 sarin [nerve gas] attack on the Tokyo subway earned them international infamy, the action still employed the most primitive of delivery systems and killed only twelve. Aum's other efforts with chemical weapons experienced problems at the delivery stage, and their biological weapons operations failed to acquire the necessary strains of bacteria. Several other difficulties confront terrorist groups looking to procure WMD from state arsenals. Considering the overwhelming military supremacy of the U.S., it is unlikely that established states would knowingly provide WMD for an attack on Americans. Given the severe military reprisal that would surely follow the discovery of such a plot, any state that sponsored terrorists would be courting regime suicide.

The national preoccupation with WMD terrorism may have more to do with emotion than rationale.

Simple Is More Deadly

It follows that poorly secured weapons in the former Soviet Union provide the most plausible, though not effortless, channel by which terrorists might achieve WMD capability, according to Warner Schilling of Columbia [University]'s Institute of War and Peace Studies. But this option still does not solve the problems of transporting and delivering chemical and biological weapons.

As for nukes, "there is the issue of bypassing the permissive action links, if any, and then designing a new detonation device. A nuclear artillery shell, for example, is not designed to go off in a shipping container," said Schilling. And to top off these obstacles, terrorists would have to overcome them while attempting to avoid detection. All this is not to say that a group with sufficient determination and resources could never develop or acquire WMD capability, but terrorists seem unlikely to dedicate the necessary resources to such endeavors when they could pursue more creative and cost-effective options with less risk of detection. The attacks of September 11 proved that box cutter-wielding hijackers can kill more Americans than the 1941 Japanese attack on Pearl Harbor. And box cutters are cheaper and easier to conceal than the hundreds of pounds of sarin that would have been necessary to achieve comparable results.

The national preoccupation with WMD terrorism may have more to do with emotion than rationale. Absolute security against any type of attack is only possible without vulnerabilities, and a society without vulnerabilities is a utopian fantasy. Instead of basing security initiatives on infinite vulnerabilities, the United States should choose an optimal set of measures based on actual threats. An overemphasis on countering WMD terrorism comes at the expense of other security measures, and an overemphasis on security as a whole comes at the expense of other national interests.

CHAPTER 2

How Can the U.S. Protect Itself Against Weapons of Mass Destruction?

Chapter Preface

During the late 1970s and early 1980s a young scientist named Peter Hagelstein worked at the Lawrence Livermore National Laboratory in California on nuclear X-ray laser technology. Hagelstein developed a theory that lasers mounted in space upon launching platforms (similar to a satellite) could be coordinated to shoot down enemy missiles launched from what was then the Soviet Union. His superior, the physicist Lowell Wood, came to believe that Hagelstein was onto something extraordinary and informed his friend, Edward Teller, a physicist and one of the developers of the atomic bomb. Teller informed President Ronald Reagan in 1983 of Hagelstein and Wood's laser-based work, leading the president to announce in a major speech that year his intent to fund advanced work on the project. The Reagan administration dubbed it the Strategic Defense Initiative (SDI). Reagan's first speech about SDI included the memorable lines: "I call upon the scientific community who gave us nuclear weapons to turn their great talents to the cause of mankind and world peace: to give us the means of rendering these nuclear weapons impotent and obsolete."

SDI was modified in theory during the administration of President George H. W. Bush into a satellite-based, mini-missile launch system to intercept incoming enemy weapons. The name was changed to Brilliant Eyes/Brilliant Pebbles, but it remained SDI in the popular press. Though the controversy regarding SDI had calmed, the defense budget still included millions of dollars to continue research into the modified SDI system.

President Bill Clinton abandoned the idea of a space-based missile defense system and withdrew its funding. However, his administration's defense budget included money to research the idea of land-based missile interceptors. According to pro–

missile defense critics, though, it was never enough money to fundamentally restructure and advance a workable system.

Immediately upon taking office in 2001, President George W. Bush committed his administration to a program named the National Missile Defense (NMD), vastly increasing defense spending and testing of the missile plan. As of early 2006 bases in Alaska and California have been stocked with interceptor missiles as the initial line of defense under the new missile defense system. The Bush administration was expected to declare the bases operational by 2005 but had not yet done so by 2006.

Simulation testing of the NMD has resulted thus far in approximately a 50 percent success ratio. Critics contend NMD is unfeasible and a waste of huge sums of budgetary dollars while supporters claim that not enough is being spent to expand NMD, not only within the United States but also to America's allies. Some foreign nations have expressed concern that the Bush administration is ultimately seeking to weaponize space under the pretense of defending the West.

There are numerous technical, political, and economic arguments surrounding the issue of a national missile defense system. The two fundamental questions, though, are: Can a missile defense system protect America from a weapons of mass destruction attack? And is it the best system to deter such an attack? These questions must be answered for *any* plan proposed to defend America. In the following viewpoints, various authors describe the necessary but different steps they believe the United States must take to protect itself from a WMD attack.

A Missile Defense System Will Protect America

Baker Spring

Baker Spring is F.M. Kirby Research Fellow in National Security Policy at the Heritage Foundation, a conservative public policy research institute in Washington, D.C.

The [George W.] Bush Administration has made great strides in ballistic missile defense [BMD] for the United States by reevaluating relevant treaties and furthering military technology. However, the threat remains. China has developed a whole new generation of mobile ICBMs [intercontinental ballistic missiles] capable of hitting the U.S., and hostile governments, such as North Korea and Iran, continue to develop and produce ballistic missiles capable of inflicting real damage upon American soil. In order to protect the U.S. from these threats, Congress should:

- Continue to improve on existing missile defense systems and interceptors;

- Support the development and deployment of sea-, land-, and space-based missile interceptors; and

- Construct a worldwide command and control system that ties together all the U.S. missile defense capabilities.

Ending Missile Vulnerability

For almost 30 years, the federal government has maintained a military posture that left the American people vulnerable to

Baker Spring, "The Operational Missile Defense Capability: A Historic Advance for the Defense of the American People," *Heritage Foundation Backgrounder #1798*, September 22, 2004. Copyright © 2004 The Heritage Foundation. Reproduced by permission.

ballistic missile attack. However, this posture of vulnerability to missile attack is about to end because the President will soon declare operational a ballistic missile defense for the American people. The earlier posture was the direct result of a policy that defined the vulnerability of the American people to missile attack as a virtue. The policy was codified in the 1972 Anti-Ballistic Missile (ABM) Treaty with the former Soviet Union.

President George W. Bush's expected declaration of an operational capability to defend the American people against a limited ballistic missile attack is, therefore, a historic achievement. The federal government is now starting to meet its obligation to defend the American people to the best of its ability.

President Bush's success marks a cardinal victory for missile defense supporters, following a long and sometimes bitter struggle. President Ronald Reagan, recognizing the moral bankruptcy and ineffectiveness of the policy of vulnerability, ended the policy in 1983. However, his Administration and the [George H.W.] Bush Administration were unable to deploy a ballistic missile defense before President Bill Clinton restored the policy of vulnerability in 1993.

The likelihood of a very destructive missile attack is higher than it was during the Cold War.

Congress terminated the policy again in 1999, and the current President Bush endorsed this decision by Congress in 2001. The difference with the current Administration, however, is that an initial missile defense capability will be declared operational and the American people will cease to be completely vulnerable to missile attack. [*Editor's note:* As of mid-2006, President Bush has not announced such an operational capability.]

The Ballistic WMD Threat

It is not a moment too soon. While today's ballistic missile threat does not portend the kind of catastrophic attack once posed by the former Soviet Union, the likelihood of a very destructive missile attack is higher than it was during the Cold War. As detailed in the findings of the 1998 commission chaired by current Secretary of Defense Donald Rumsfeld, a larger number of states, some governed by unpredictable leaders, are obtaining ballistic missiles and the nuclear, chemical, and biological warheads to arm them.

This rampant proliferation of ballistic missiles and weapons of mass destruction makes the world less predictable and stable than it was during the Cold War. These threats include missiles like the North Korean Taepo Dong-2, the Chinese DF-41, and the Russian SS-27, whether launched deliberately or by accident. Further, virtually all of today's missile powers are modernizing their arsenals. For example, press reports from early August indicate that North Korea is deploying new land-based and sea-based ballistic missiles based on a decommissioned Soviet missile. . . .

A Battle over Ideology

There is no denying that the debate over missile defense, both domestically in the U.S. and internationally in the West, was driven by ideological differences. It is not coincidental that opponents of missile defense in the West generally adhered to a larger foreign policy that sought to find accommodation with the Soviet Union and also tended to support socialist policies at home. These opponents tended to make arguments of moral equivalency between the democratic and free-market economic policies of the U.S. and the communist ideology of the former Soviet Union. For example, the historians Leslie Adler and Thomas Paterson are quoted stating that Soviet Communism was a "system proclaiming a humanistic ideology," which "failed[ed] to live up to its ideal."

Further, this same group favored domestic policies that would have imposed greater government control on the economy and shrink the private sector both economically and socially. Ultimately, these policies sought to blur the distinctions between Western and Soviet domestic policies and were propped up by wildly inaccurate claims about the strength of the Soviet economy. Clearly, those in favor of these policies were grouped on the liberal side of the ideological spectrum. . . .

Conservatives supported the policies of individual liberty and market economies and did not accept the assertion that the Soviet system pointed to social progress. They accepted the ideological confrontation with the Soviet Union and wanted to prevail in this contest.

Conservatives therefore agreed with liberals that missile defense represented a tool for confronting the Soviet Union, as well as a means for confounding the Soviet strategy of relying on military threats to subdue the West. In the view of conservatives, the accumulation of military power was the Soviet Union's strongest card in seeking to spread its ideology and project power. They saw high technology defense systems, including missile defenses, as an important means of addressing this Soviet strength.

Supporters of missile defense . . . sought the expansion of U.S. power . . . as necessary to preserving Western values and liberty.

From today's perspective, after the collapse of Communism in 1989 and the Soviet Union in 1991, it is difficult to fathom that the liberal position was the dominant one in Washington from the late 1960s until the early 1980s. Clearly, the events of the late 1980s and early 1990s discredited the ideological underpinnings of the liberal opposition to missile defense. Nevertheless, the policy of vulnerability was so firmly entrenched that it would take another decade before the U.S. would be in a position to put even a limited missile defense system in place.

Defining American Power

If ideological differences were at the core of the debate in the U.S. over missile defense, differing views regarding world politics ran a close second. Particularly at the outset of the Cold War, when the Soviet Union had yet to recover from the effects of World War II, some in the West warned against a U.S. that had accumulated too much power. They saw this earlier "unipolar world"—to use the term coined by [conservative columnist] Charles Krauthammer to describe today's world—as inherently unstable. In this context, they saw U.S. vulnerability as an appropriate limit on its power.

In essence, this group quietly welcomed Soviet acquisition of atomic and thermonuclear weaponry as a counterbalance to U.S. power. . . .

Supporters of missile defense, by contrast, did not harbor doubts about an excess of U.S. power. In fact, they sought the expansion of U.S. power—President Reagan referred to it as operating from a position of strength—as necessary to preserving Western values and liberty.

While missile defense supporters were not advocating needlessly provocative or risky actions toward the Soviet Union, neither did they seek a permanent stalemate. They wanted to prevail. Further, they did not accept the underlying technical argument that missile defenses would create an incentive for a first strike and were destabilizing. Quite the opposite: They saw the policy of vulnerability and the absence of missile defenses as facilitating Soviet first strike options for destroying the U.S. retaliatory capacity. . . .

Missile Defense Will Not Lead to an Arms Race

Missile defense opponents of almost every stripe strongly held the view that missile defenses and strategic nuclear arms control were incompatible. This view was based on the assumption that missile defenses would lead inevitably to an arms race spurred by a dynamic where each increment of defense would be offset by an additional increment of offense and vice versa.

President Bush proved that the missile defense critics' assumption was erroneous in the course of 2001 and 2002. First, President Bush announced at the White House on December 13, 2001, that the U.S. was withdrawing from the ABM Treaty. This step cleared the way for unfettered development and deployment of an effective missile defense system. Second, he signed a strategic nuclear arms reduction treaty with Russian President Vladimir Putin in Moscow on May 24, 2002. This treaty will reduce the number of deployed strategic nuclear warheads on each side to between 1,700 and 2,200. This is down from Cold War highs of well in excess of 10,000 on each side. . . .

Missile defense proponents have no choice but to press forward with additional numbers and kinds of missile defense systems.

Catching Up to the Threat

Monumental efforts and achievements by their nature frequently do not yield immediate practical benefits. Rather, the practical benefits accrue over time. This is the case with missile defense because such systems cannot be developed and deployed on short notice, even with a clear mandate.

Given the enormous achievement of the Bush Administration in bringing the missile defense program to the point that an operational defense capability can be deployed, it is important for missile defense supporters to recognize that this achievement is perishable. This is because the initial operational capability is limited. The failure to improve and strengthen it will raise questions about the value of having it at all. The last time the U.S. fielded such a capability, in the mid-1970s, it was shut down almost immediately. This was because it became clear that the limited capability was not going to be improved and that the military and political value of having the system was open to question.

Augmenting the initial missile defense capability is necessary to catch up with and surpass the developing missile threat.

The lesson here is that missile defense proponents have no choice but to press forward with additional numbers and kinds of missile defense systems. During the almost 30 years that the U.S. denied itself missile defenses, the missile threat was advancing. President Bush has brought the U.S. to the point that it is now catching up with the threat. The next step is to surpass the threat and limit the choices of those who would threaten the U.S. with missile attack.

The limited capability of the initial missile defense system is revealed by the fact that it is described as a "Test Bed." The purpose of the Test Bed is twofold: It will provide the initial operational capability and the means to develop and test more effective defenses. Lieutenant General Ronald T. Kadish, former Missile Defense Agency (MDA) director, succinctly described the rationale behind this approach in congressional testimony [in] spring [2004]:

> When we put [the ballistic missile defense] system on alert, we will have a capability that we currently do not have. In my opinion, a capability against even a single reentry vehicle [warhead] has significant military utility. Even that modest

defensive capability will help reduce the more immediate threats to our security and enhance our ability to defend our interests abroad. We also may cause adversaries of the United States to rethink their investments in ballistic missiles.

The Initial Missile Defense System

The initial ballistic missile defense capability will consist of the following components:

- Up to 20 ground-based interceptors at Fort Greely, Alaska, and Vandenberg Air Force Base, California (with six interceptors in place at Fort Greely by the end of 2004);

- An upgraded Cobra Dane radar at Eareckson Air Station in Alaska;

- Upgraded early warning radar in California and the United Kingdom;

- Three BMD-capable Aegis cruisers with up to 10 SM-3 missiles to be available by the end of 2005; and

- Ten Aegis destroyers, modified with improved SPY-1 radars by the end of 2005 (with an additional five destroyers by 2006).

The interceptors used in this initial capability are ground-based midcourse interceptors. They will be based in silos and can destroy incoming ballistic missiles during the midcourse stage of flight (when the missiles are in space).

Why the Bush Administration chose to place the initial interceptors in Alaska becomes clear when the location of the Alaska site is compared to the flight trajectories of the most likely near-term purposeful or accidental launches of long-range missiles against the U.S. The comparison clearly shows that the Alaska site is optimized for countering North Korea's long-range missile threat, which is the most immediate among the regimes most hostile to the U.S. According to testimony by former Director of Central Intelligence George Tenet before the Senate Intelligence Committee on February 24, [2004,] the North Korean Taepo Dong-2, a long-range missile, is capable of delivering a nuclear warhead to U.S. territory and is ready for flight testing at any time.

Creating the Future Missile Defense

By the same token, the Alaska site is not optimized for countering the emerging Iranian missile threat. This is why augmenting the initial missile defense capability is necessary to catch up with and surpass the developing missile threat. Deploying additional interceptors and sensors located and oriented to address the Iranian threat is one of the means of addressing this problem.

Further, the Alaska site is not designed to address the threat of shorter-range missiles launched from ships near the U.S. coast. This is why the initial capability will include three Aegis cruisers carrying 10 SM-3 interceptor missiles. These interceptors will give the military at least a chance to counter this threat, which the 1998 Rumsfeld Commission cited as a serious concern. These sea-based interceptors, along with the Patriot system for intercepting shorter-range missiles in the terminal phase of flight, can also defend U.S. friends and allies and U.S. troops deployed abroad.

A Missile Defense System Will Not Protect America

Charles V. Peña

Charles V. Peña is the director of defense policy studies at the Cato Institute, a libertarian research organization in Washington, D.C.

The need for missile defense is often based on a "doom and gloom" picture painted by its advocates. For example, James Anderson at the Heritage Foundation states that "ballistic missiles are capable of destroying life and property on a massive scale. . . . Yet our country remains naked to these missiles." He further states that "*every American already is a hostage to the threat of missile attack.*" When President [George W.] Bush announced that the United States would withdraw from the Anti-Ballistic Missile [ABM] Treaty, he said that "the ABM treaty hinders our government's ability to develop ways to protect our people from future terrorist or rogue state missile attacks" and that "defending the American people is my highest priority as Commander in Chief, and I cannot and will not allow the United States to remain in a treaty that prevents us from developing effective defenses."

[In 2003] CIA director George Tenet responded in the affirmative when asked on Capitol Hill whether North Korea currently has a missile capable of hitting the West Coast of the United States. The doomsayers were quick to proclaim that Americans are defenseless against the dire threat posed by North Korea's two nuclear warheads.

Charles V. Peña, "Missile Defense: Defending America or Building Empire?" *Cato Institute Foreign Policy Briefing*, no. 77, May 28, 2003, pp. 6–11. Copyright © 2003 CATO Institute. All rights reserved. Reproduced by permission.

The Real Reason for Missile Defense

In other words, the purpose of missile defense is supposed to be to protect the American people. But the rhetoric conceals the real reason for missile defense. According to the Missile Defense Agency [MDA] the Department of Defense organization responsible for developing a missile defense system, "The fundamental goal of the planned BMD [Ballistic Missile Defense] system is to defend the forces and territories of the United States, its Allies, and friends as soon as practicable." Thus, the purpose of missile defense is extended well beyond protecting America and Americans.

That is why the MDA is pursuing a layered missile defense system "capable of engaging all classes of ballistic missile threats." The direct threat to the U.S. homeland is posed by ICBMs [intercontinental ballistic missiles], which are currently possessed by only the United States, Russia, and China. Because of its militarily secure geostrategic position, other types of shorter range ballistic missiles do not pose a threat to the United States—but are threats to foreign friends and allies. Perhaps the clearest indication that defending the United States is not necessarily the primary objective of a future missile defense system is this statement by the MDA about the threat: "The proliferation of weapons of mass destruction and the ballistic and cruise missiles that could deliver them pose a direct and immediate threat to the security of *U.S. military forces and assets in overseas theaters of operation, our allies and friends*, as well as our own country."

Space-based [missile defense] capability would inherently provide global coverage well beyond defending [America].

Adding Space Weapons

That is also the reason for wanting to develop a space-based boost phase intercept capability. Boost phase is defined as the portion of a missile's flight from launch to breaking free of the earth's gravitational forces. Depending on the range of the missile, boost phase lasts between three and five minutes. For longer range missiles the rocket will actually exit the earth's atmosphere into outer space; for shorter range missiles the rocket will reach only the fringes of outer space. Because of the dynamics of missile flight and the relatively short engagement time for intercept, the best way to achieve boost phase intercept is from space based platforms that can shoot downward at a launching missile rather than from the ground shooting upward. The MDA fiscal year 2004–05 budget estimate does not specify how much money will be allocated to space based defense, but it does state that the agency "will initiate a space-based Test Bed development to determine the feasibility of exploiting the inherent advantages of intercepting threat missiles from space" and "begin developing a space-based kinetic energy interceptor in FY04 [fiscal year 2004], with initial, on-orbit testing to commence with three to five satellites in Block 2008 [a two-year block of time related to funding]." It had previously been reported that MDA proposed to spend $54 million on space-based kinetic energy kill vehicle concepts and was seeking $634 million for directed-energy weapons, including research and development of a space-based laser.

To be sure, there are many operational advantages to being able to intercept a missile in its boost phase—for example, a single effective shot could kill a missile carrying multiple warheads before any decoys or countermeasure could be deployed. If the missile were carrying a chemical or biological weapon, the debris would most likely fall on the country that launched the missile. But the other reason boost-phase intercept is wanted is because a space-based capability would inherently provide global coverage well beyond defending against only those ballistic missiles that directly threaten the United States. According to the Heritage Foundation's Commission on Missile Defense, "A missile defense system should be global in nature" and "the fastest and least expensive way to build a global missile defense system would be to begin by building sea-based defenses and then to *follow them as soon as possible with space-based defenses.*"

Protecting U.S. Forces by Missile Defense

So it's not really defending America against ICBMs—missiles that rogue states currently don't have and aren't likely to develop or deploy for perhaps a decade or more—that is driving the push for missile defense. Rather, the real rationale for missile defense is to protect U.S. forces so they can engage in military intervention throughout the world. Such thinking is not set forth in the new national security strategy, but it is explicit in a document many consider a "blueprint" and inspiration for the new strategy, *Rebuilding America's Defenses* by the Project of the New American Century published in September 2000. Ordinarily, such a report might be dismissed as just another Washington, "inside the beltway" policy exercise. But many of the project participants [later sat] in influential positions either inside the Bush administration or as advisers to the administration. . . .

The real ballistic missile threat is the shorter-range missile . . . that rogue states already have.

According to *Rebuilding America's Defenses*:

- "[The United States must] develop and deploy *global missile defenses* to defend the American homeland and American allies, and *to provide a secure basis for U.S. power protection around the world.*"

- "Effective ballistic missile defenses will be the central element in the exercise of American power and the projection of U.S. military forces abroad."

- "The failure to build missile defenses will . . . compromise the exercise of American power abroad."

Thus, the real ballistic missile threat is the shorter-range missiles (like Scuds) that rogue states already have. According to the NIC [National Intelligence Council], "The threats to the U.S. homeland, nevertheless, will consist of dramatically fewer warheads than today owing to significant reductions in Russian strategic forces." So the ballistic missile threat against America is actually decreasing. Conversely, the NIC states that "short- and medium-range ballistic missiles, particularly if armed with WMD [weapons of mass destruction], already pose a significant threat overseas to US interests, military forces, and allies." Furthermore, "Emerging ballistic missile states continue to increase the range, reliability, and accuracy of the missile systems in their inventories—posing ever greater risks to US forces, interests, and allies throughout the world." At most, only two potentially hostile countries (Russia and China) possess ballistic missiles capable of striking the United States. The Pentagon, however, claims 28 threat countries (without naming them specifically) with ballistic missiles, but those missile systems are all short or medium range.

Chasing Military Superiority

Why the great concern about ballistic missiles that cannot reach the United States? Because [to again quote from *Rebuilding America's Defenses:*]

> Weak states operating small arsenals of crude ballistic missiles, armed with basic nuclear warheads or other weapons of mass destruction, will be in a strong position to deter the United States from using conventional force, no matter the technological or other advantages we may enjoy. Even if such enemies are merely able to threaten American allies rather than the United States homeland itself, America's ability to project power will be deeply compromised.

So missile defense is arguably more about the ability to use conventional offensive force throughout the world than about defending the American homeland.

And the purpose of conventional force superiority around the globe is to "preserve and enhance this 'American peace.'" Of course, the new national security strategy is not quite so blunt and states that "the presence of American forces overseas is one of the most profound symbols of the U.S. commitments to allies and friends. Through our willingness to use force in our own defense and in defense of others, the United States demonstrates its resolve to maintain a balance of power that favors freedom." Indeed, the new national security strategy calls for making the world "better" by "expanding liberty" throughout the world on the basis of American values of "political and economic freedom, peaceful relations with other states, and respect for human dignity." Regardless of how it is dressed up, that is a strategy of American empire. And, ultimately, that is what missile defense is all about.

Fueling Anti-Americanism

But what never seems to occur to advocates of a strategy of empire is that the result will be increased resentment of and animosity toward what is perceived by the rest of the world as an imperialist America. It is popular to think that other countries and people hate the United States for "who we are." In his address to a joint session of Congress and the American people after the September 11 [2001] terrorist attacks, President Bush said: "Why do they hate us? They hate what we see right here in this chamber—a democratically elected government. . . . They hate our freedoms—our freedom of religion, our freedom of speech, our freedom to vote and assemble and disagree with each other." To be sure, radical Islamists may have a deep-seated hatred for the United States. But the reality that is largely ignored is that U.S. policies and actions are significant factors in triggering terrorist attacks;

those factors go beyond any hatred of America, its culture, and its values. . . .

The strategy of empire is simply the old Cold War strategy run amok and without a Soviet enemy. A better alternative is for the United States to adopt a more restrained foreign policy—sometimes called minimalist realism, off-shore balancer, or balancer of last resort. This is not a call for isolationism or "Fortress America" but simple recognition that the United States does not have to be the world's policeman (or armed social worker) and intercede in the myriad problems and conflicts that arise around the world. Whereas empire seeks to impose U.S. will and dictate outcomes, it is more prudent and realistic to recognize and accept that even a country as large and powerful as the United States cannot control what happens everywhere in the world.

U.S. security no longer depends on an expansive, forward-deployed defense perimeter.

More important, the United States does not *need* to control outcomes everywhere and on every issue. In the post–Cold War world with no strategic peer competitor and no would-be hegemonic power on the horizon, the United States is in a unique, secure geostrategic position. Friendly neighbors to the north and south and vast oceans to the east and west make a large-scale conventional military attack highly implausible. And the vast U.S. strategic arsenal serves as an effective deterrent against the use of nuclear weapons by any hostile nation. So every problem, crisis, and conflict in the world is not a direct threat to vital U.S. security interests. Put another way, U.S. security no longer depends on an expansive, forward-deployed defense perimeter. And instead of being an intervener of first resort, the United States should be the balancer of last resort and step in only when its vital interests are at stake. The most vital interest, of course, is the homeland.

An Obsolete Strategy

Such a change in security strategy and policy is even more appropriate, given the threat of terrorism. As Ted Galen Carpenter of the Cato Institute points out: "Making that change would have been wise even before the events of September 11. The terrorist attacks on America have given added urgency to the need to adjust Washington's security policy. . . . We cannot afford the distraction of maintaining increasingly obsolete and irrelevant security commitments around the globe." A changed national security strategy would come directly to grips with the fact that, since terrorist attacks are virtually impossible to deter, prevent, or mitigate, U.S. security would be better served by not engaging in unnecessary military deployments and interventions that fuel the flames of vehement anti-American sentiment.

The truth is that the ballistic missile threat posed by rogue states is relatively limited.

Given such a strategy and to the extent that a missile defense is technically feasible, proven to be operationally effective (via realistic testing, including against decoys and countermeasures), and affordable, a limited land-based ballistic missile defense system designed to protect the U.S. homeland makes sense. After all, that is the primary responsibility of the federal government. But it is not the responsibility of the United States to protect friends and allies, especially when many of them are wealthy enough to pay for their own missile defense if they think it's important for their own security.

The truth is that the ballistic missile threat posed by rogue states is relatively limited. And any defense expenditure—including spending on missile defense—must be commensurate with the threat. Therefore, a limited threat—albeit potentially destructive—deserves only limited public resources to counter it. The vast U.S. strategic nuclear arsenal would likely serve as a strong deterrent against any intentional attack. But a limited and truly "national" missile defense system would be a good backup—or insurance policy—against the low likelihood of an accidental or unauthorized launch by a nuclear power or if deterrence failed against a rogue state.

A global missile defense to protect friends, allies, and U.S. forces abroad may provide a false sense of security.

A False Sense of Security

It would seem that the Bush administration and advocates of missile defense have successfully used rhetoric about needing missile defense to protect Americans who are defenseless against ballistic missile attack to justify increased spending and a planned initial deployment at Fort Greely, Alaska. . . . But in reality missile defense is about defending U.S. forces deployed in an ever-expanding security perimeter around the world, ostensibly to defend freedom.

Pursuing such an expansive global missile defense to support a strategy of empire would not only be expensive and technically difficult and complex—indeed, building any missile defense system will be the most technically complex and challenging weapon system ever—but downright dangerous.

No weapon system is 100 percent perfect. Missile defense will not be any different. Therefore, no missile defense system can guarantee that all incoming warheads will be destroyed. As a result, a global missile defense to protect friends, allies, and U.S. forces abroad may provide a false sense of security. Policymakers pursuing a strategy of empire and willing to take preemptive military action might be emboldened to engage in risky military interventions overseas. If adversaries feel they have nothing to lose (and are armed with long-range ballistic missiles and WMD), they might decide to launch an attack against the United States (although they would otherwise be deterred from doing so if not provoked by a U.S. attack). Given a less than perfect missile defense, the possibility of a warhead getting through would be very real. A potentially catastrophic attack on U.S. soil (a failure of the first magnitude in U.S. national security policy) could thus result from unneeded U.S. military action against a country that would not have directly threatened the United States if it had been left alone.

Ultimately, the global missile defense sought by the administration is a shield for a quixotic crusade using military force to build a safer and better world based on American values. But that strategy will have the perverse effect of making the United States less secure by sowing the seeds of hate and vehement anti-American sentiment under the guise of expanding liberty. Such actions could result in more terrorist recruits and terrorist violence. And a missile defense, no matter how effective, will not protect Americans from terrorists using easier and cheaper means to inflict mass casualties—witness 9/11 [2001].

Censoring Scientific Work Will Help Fight Bioterrorism

Jeremy Marwell

Jeremy Marwell is a research associate in science and technology studies at the Council on Foreign Relations in New York City.

In this age of terror, when should science silence itself?

Apparently, now. In an extraordinary coalition against bioterrorism, 32 editors from *Nature, Science* and other leading journals in the United States and Britain have committed themselves to altering or refusing to publish the tiny fraction of papers submitted to them that could compromise security. At stake: data or results that might help terrorists use toxins or viruses as biological weapons.

The critics were quick to weigh in. How, they ask, can scientists distinguish harmful information from the innocuous? How can scientific careers and science itself advance under such a gag order? And more practically, can editors at a few elite journals really halt the flow of terrorizing information in the Internet age?

But voluntary self-censorship not only can help make us secure, it also will forestall government from censoring in a more heavy-handed way. This, isn't the first time U.S. scientists have faced the need for self-censorship.

Censoring the Atomic Bomb Data

In May 1940, eight months after the outbreak of war in Europe, the U.S. physicist Gregory Breit undertook a nearly single-handed effort to halt publication of scientific articles in the newly discovered field of nuclear fission. Like many of his

Jeremy Marwell, "In Bad Days, Science Must Muzzle Itself," *Los Angeles Times*, March 4, 2003. Reproduced by permission.

colleagues, Breit believed that research on fission in the uranium nucleus could lead to weapons of unprecedented destructive power. At the time, with Americans loath to enter a distant war even as Hitler marched across Europe, the U.S. government had shown little interest in official control or censorship of American fission publications.

Working with the tacit approval of President Franklin D. Roosevelt's secret "Uranium Committee," Breit persuaded editors at leading U.S. and British physics journals to delay publication of sensitive material about uranium until after the war. To decide which papers would require this status, Breit established a small reference committee composed of some of the top nuclear physicists, including current and future Nobel laureates Harold Urey, Eugene Wigner and Enrico Fermi.

Until the advent in 1942 of the Manhattan Project [to build the atomic bomb], which imposed tight military secrecy on sensitive uranium research and eliminated the need for self-restraint, Breit's committee reviewed and withheld dozens of papers. Among the topics deemed too sensitive for publication were uranium isotope separation and neutron dynamics, two crucial aspects in engineering an atomic bomb. These efforts kept sensitive information from German nuclear scientists.

One recent [scientific] paper ... would have revealed how to modify a microbe so that it could kill 1 million people.

Preventing the Leak of Dangerous Information

Today's quandary is, of course, far greater than the one scientists faced in the early 1940s, when the most crucial topics were narrowly linked to uranium. Breit's effort, however, can offer lessons for today's war on bioterrorism, where the scope and diversity of potentially sensitive topics are far greater.

Imperfect action is better than doing nothing at all. In May 1940, Breit realized that every paper published would lead Germany closer to a nuclear bomb. Cobbling together a hasty, informal consensus, Breit did not wait for a congressional or presidential mandate. He simply began persuading editors.

Today, we know that terrorist groups at home and abroad are interested in biological and chemical weapons. So the editors' plan, whatever its shortcomings, at least assures that blatant cases will be filtered out. One recent paper, withheld from publication by the American Society of Microbiology, would have revealed how to modify a microbe so that it could kill 1 million people instead of 10,000.

Timeliness, expertise and flexibility must be watchwords as science strikes a balance between openness and prudence.

Self-Censorship Is Better than Government Censorship

Open publication is the lifeblood of science, conferring authorship and precedence on individual scientists and allowing the scientific community to duplicate and verify discoveries. As a physicist, Breit recognized the crucial importance of publishing whenever possible. His panel struggled to distinguish between "pure science" and results that might have dangerous implications or applications.

Similarly, today's approach places journal editors, who have a personal and professional stake in maintaining open scientific dialogue, in a central role. Imagine the alternative: a government-mandated program, perhaps including the creeping authorities of the military and intelligence services, likely to err toward excessive secrecy in the name of national security.

Timeliness, expertise and flexibility must be watchwords as science strikes a balance between openness and prudence. The scientific editors have struck the right note. It is now up to the rest of the peaceful scientific community, both here and in centers of biological innovation abroad, to follow suit.

A Healthy Public Infrastructure Is the Best Defense Against Bioterrorism

Naomi Klein

Naomi Klein is an internationally syndicated columnist for the Globe and Mail *in Canada and the* Guardian *in Great Britain.*

Only hours after the [2001] terrorist attacks on the World Trade Center and the Pentagon, Republican Representative Curt Weldon went on CNN and announced that he didn't want to hear anyone talking about funding for schools or hospitals. From here on, it was all about spies, bombs and other manly things.

"The first priority of the U.S. government is not education, it is not health care, it is the defense and protection of U.S. citizens," he said, adding, later: "I'm a teacher married to a nurse—none of that matters today."

But now it turns out that those frivolous social services matter a great deal. What is making the U.S. most vulnerable to terrorist networks is not a depleted weapons arsenal but its starved, devalued and crumbling public sector. The new battlefields are not just the Pentagon, but also the post office; not just military intelligence, but also training for doctors and nurses; not a sexy new missile defense shield, but the boring old Food and Drug Administration [FDA].

A Decayed Public Health System

It has become fashionable to wryly observe that the terrorists use the West's technologies as weapons against itself: planes, e-mail, cellphones. But as fears of bioterrorism mount, it could well turn out that their best weapons are the rips and-holes in the United States' public infrastructure.

Is this because there was no time to prepare for the attacks? Hardly. The U.S. has openly recognized the threat of biological attacks since the [1991] Persian Gulf war, and Bill Clinton renewed calls to protect the nation from bioterror after the 1998 embassy bombings in East Africa. And yet shockingly little has been done.

Many doctors in the U.S. public health-care system have not been trained to identify symptoms of anthrax, botulism or plague.

The reason is simple: Preparing for biological warfare would have required a ceasefire in America's older, less dramatic war—the one against the public sphere. It didn't happen. Here are some snapshots from the front lines.

The health system: Half the states in the U.S. don't have federal experts trained in bioterrorism. The Centers for Disease Control and Prevention are buckling under the strain of anthrax fears, their underfunded labs scrambling to keep up with the demand for tests. Little research has been done on how to treat children who have contracted anthrax, since Cipro—the most popular antibiotic [for anthrax]—is not recommended [for children].

Many doctors in the U.S. public health-care system have not been trained to identify symptoms of anthrax, botulism or plague. A recent U.S. Senate panel heard that hospitals and health departments lack basic diagnostic tools, and information sharing is difficult since some departments don't have e-mail access. Many health departments are closed on weekends, with no staff on call.

An Overwhelmed Public Health System

If treatment is a mess, federal inoculation programs are in worse shape. The only laboratory in the U.S. licensed to produce the anthrax vaccine has left the country unprepared for its current crisis. Why? It's a typical privatization debacle. The lab, in Lansing, Mich., used to be owned and operated by the state. In 1998, it was sold to BioPort, which promised greater efficiency. The new lab has failed several FDA inspections and, so far, has been unable to supply a single dose of the vaccine to the U.S. military, let alone to the general population.

As for smallpox, there are not nearly enough vaccines to cover the population, leading the U.S. National Institute of Allergy and Infectious Diseases to experiment with diluting the existing vaccines at a ratio of 1 to 5 or even 1 to 10.

The Water System internal documents show that the U.S. Environmental Protection Agency [EPA] is years behind schedule in safeguarding the water supply against bioterrorist attacks. According to an audit released on Oct. 4, [2001,] the EPA was supposed to have identified security vulnerabilities in municipal water supplies by 1999, but it hasn't yet completed even this first stage.

What 'homeland security' really means is a mad rush to reassemble basic public infrastructure . . . and health and safety standards.

The food supply: The FDA has proved unable to introduce measures that would better protect the food supply from "agroterrorism"—deadly bacteria introduced to the food supply. With agriculture increasingly centralized and globalized, the sector is vulnerable to the spread of disease, both inside the U.S. and outside (as the [2001] hoof-and-mouth epidemic [in British cattle] demonstrated . . .). But the FDA, which inspected only 1 per cent of food imports under its jurisdiction [in 2000], says it is in "desperate need of more inspectors."

Tom Hammonds, CEO of the Food Marketing Institute, an industry group representing food sellers, says, "Should a crisis arise—real or manufactured as a hoax—the deficiencies of the current system would become glaringly obvious."

Public Health Is a Security Issue

After Sept. 11, [2001,] George W. Bush created the position of "homeland security," designed to evoke a nation steeled and prepared for any attack. And yet it turns out that what "homeland security" really means is a mad rush to reassemble basic public infrastructure and resurrect health and safety standards that have been drastically eroded. The troops at the front lines of America's new war are embattled, indeed: the very bureaucracies that have been cut back, privatized and vilified for two decades, not just in the U.S. but in virtually every country in the world.

"Public health is a national security issue," U.S. Secretary of Health Tommy Thompson observed [in October 2001]. No kidding. For years, critics have argued that there are human costs to all the cost-cutting, deregulating and privatizing—train crashes in Britain, E. coli outbreaks in Walkerton [Ontario], food poisoning, and substandard health care. And yet until Sept. 11, [2001,] "security" was still narrowly confined to the machinery of war and policing, a fortress built atop a crumbling foundation.

If there is a lesson to be learned, it is that real security cannot be cordoned off. It is woven into our most basic social fabric, from the post office to the emergency room, from the subway to the water reservoir, from schools to food inspection. Infrastructure—the boring stuff that binds us all together—is not irrelevant to the serious business of fighting terrorism. It is the foundation of our future security.

The United States Should Hold Foreign Nations Accountable for Nuclear Terrorism

Michael A. Levi

Michael A. Levi is a physicist and a fellow in foreign policy studies at the Brookings Institution in Washington, D.C.

Has terrorism made deterrence obsolete? President [George W.] Bush articulated the prevailing view in his June 2002 West Point address: "Deterrence—the promise of massive retaliation against nations—means nothing against shadowy terrorist networks with no nation or citizens to defend. Containment is not possible when unbalanced dictators with weapons of mass destruction can deliver those weapons on missiles or secretly provide them to terrorist allies." Debate over missile defense aside, U.S. foreign policy thinkers have largely accepted his reasoning, though they argue on the margins over how unbalanced most dictators are.

Yet in confronting the prospect of nuclear terrorism—and there is no more dire threat facing America today—this logic is flawed. Its purported truth in addressing nuclear terror relies almost entirely on its assumption that rogue states could provide nuclear weapons "secretly" to terrorists. But were such now-secret links to be exposed, deterrence could largely be restored. The United States would threaten unacceptable retaliation were a state to provide the seeds of a terrorist nuclear attack; unable to use terrorists for clandestine delivery, rogue states would be returned to the grim reality of massive retaliation.

Most policymakers have assumed that exposing such links would be impossible. It is not. Building on scientific tech-

Michael A. Levi, "Deterring Nuclear Terrorism," *Issues in Science and Technology Online*, Spring 2004. Reproduced by permission.

niques developed during the Cold War, the United States stands a good chance of developing the tools needed to attribute terrorist nuclear attacks to their state sponsors. If it can put those tools in place and let its enemies know of their existence, deterrence could become one of the most valuable tools in the war on terror.

Breaking the Terror–Rogue State Connection

Terrorists cannot build nuclear weapons without first acquiring fissile materials—plutonium or highly enriched uranium—from a state source. They might steal materials from poorly secured stockpiles in the former Soviet Union, but with the right investment in cooperative threat reduction, that possibility can be precluded. Alternatively, they could acquire fissile materials from a sympathetic, or desperate, state source. North Korea presented this threat most acutely when it threatened in May 2003 to sell plutonium to the highest bidder.

We must learn to identify a nuclear weapon's origin after it has exploded, by examining its residue.

The Bush administration appears to be acutely aware of such a possibility and is trying to prevent it by fighting state-based nuclear proliferation and by attempting to eliminate terrorist groups. Yet it has taken few effective steps to break direct connections between terrorists and nuclear rogues. The elimination of terrorist networks and prevention of nuclear proliferation should be top goals, but a robust policy cannot be predicated on assuming universal success in those two endeavors.

Two basic lines of attack might help break any connection. In the one currently favored by the administration, militaries attempt to break the terrorist/state link physically by focusing on interdiction of nuclear weapons transfers. But the technical barriers to such a strategy's success are high. A grapefruit-sized ball of plutonium or a cantaloupe's worth of highly enriched uranium is enough for a crude nuclear weapon that would flatten much of a city, and detecting such a shipment would be extremely difficult. Like missile defense, interdiction is a useful tool in preventing nuclear attack, but also like missile defense, it is far from sufficient in itself. In confronting the threat of missile attack, the United States ultimately relies on deterrence, threatening any would-be attacker with unacceptable punishment. It will need the same tool to prevent nuclear terrorism.

Deterring nuclear terror by threatening its . . . sponsors [would use] retribution not as an end but as a means to prevent attacks.

An Unsettling Solution

This, of course, begs a question: If nuclear materials are so hard to detect, how can state/terrorist connections be exposed? Solving this problem requires a novel and somewhat unsettling twist. Instead of simply focusing on intercepting bombs, we must learn to identify a nuclear weapon's origin after it has exploded, by examining its residue. If the United States can take that technical step, it can credibly assure its enemies that their transfer of weapons to terrorists will ultimately lead to their demise.

At first glance, such a strategy might appear foolish: It would provide little comfort to identify an attack's perpetrator after a U.S. city has already been destroyed. Adopting this criticism, though, would miss the essence of deterrence. During the Cold War, U.S. deterrence was based firmly in its ability to retaliate after a devastating Soviet attack. This by no means suggested that such an attack was acceptable or that retaliation would provide comfort. Instead, what was important was the threat's ability to discourage any attack from occurring in the first place. Similarly, deterring nuclear terror by threatening its would-be sponsors would be aimed at using retribution not as an end but as a means to prevent attacks.

Finding the Source

Finding a successful deterrence strategy requires that we make retaliatory action as certain as possible; there must be little room for the adversary to gamble that it might transfer nuclear weapons without suffering. Ideally, the United States would identify nuclear transfers when they occurred and punish the participants accordingly. However, the difficulty of intercepting nuclear transfers might embolden enemies to attempt to evade such a system. Moreover, enemies might believe that even if a transfer were detected, the United States would lack the resolve to punish them. Pyongyang [North Korea's capital], for example, with more than 10,000 artillery pieces poised for counterattack against Seoul [South Korea's capital], might conclude that the United States would not follow through on its retaliatory threats were it to intercept a North Korean bomb that had not yet been detonated.

To successfully attribute an attack, there must be a state fingerprint to match it to.

Focusing on actual attacks rather than on transfers would solve both of these problems. Few doubt the U.S. resolve to retaliate were a nuclear bomb to be detonated in a U.S. city. And unlike shadowy transfers of nuclear material, a nuclear attack would surely be noticed.

The missing link, which scientists must provide, is the ability to attribute a nuclear weapon to its state source after an attack. On its face, this might appear impossible—during a nuclear detonation, the weapon's fissile core of plutonium or uranium would be vaporized and transmuted, flung outward with the force of 20,000 tons of TNT. And yet, surprisingly, such a cataclysmic event would still leave behind traces from which the original bomb's characteristics might be reconstructed.

Building on the Past

Already, scientists at the nation's three principal nuclear weapons laboratories are working on the problem. They have decades of experience to build on. Before 1963, when the world ceased testing nuclear weapons in the atmosphere, the United States developed techniques to infer details of Soviet bombs by examining their fallout, which they could detect from far away. By positing a range of possible bomb designs, technicians could infer details about the fissile materials—plutonium, or uranium—used in the Soviet bombs, along with some of the weapons' design details. (Presumably, the Soviets did the same to spy on the United States; thus, the two countries might cooperate to further develop attribution abilities.) Some of that expertise is still maintained, particularly in the conjunction with the Nuclear Emergency Search Teams, whose task is to respond to nuclear terrorist incidents. Building on that foundation will require training a new generation of scientists in forensic techniques that were abandoned long ago. It will also require an effort by laboratory scientists to imagine weapon designs that terrorists or rogues might use. (Such designs could be simulated using the Department of Energy's Advanced Supercomputing Initiative and would not require nuclear testing to validate.) It would be wise to pursue much of this in a limited multilateral environment, thus helping reassure the world that our attributions are sound and unbiased.

Fingerprinting Weapons

By itself, however, the ability to infer a bomb's composition will not be enough. To successfully attribute an attack, there must be a state fingerprint to match it to. Knowing any characteristics of enemy weapons will be useful, but it will be particularly helpful to know the finer details of others' plutonium and uranium. Those two elements come in various isotopes [atomic forms], and a given sample of either metal will combine several of those isotopes in hard-to-alter combinations. To some degree, one can infer those characteristics from the design details of the enemy's production facilities and from the operating histories of its plants. In other cases, such as in Korea in the 1990s, special access [through International Atomic Energy Agency investigations] will make it possible to measure the composition of a country's uranium or plutonium. If the isotopic details of a weapon are known, attributing it will be much easier.

It may be possible to go further by exploiting states' interest in not being wrongly identified as having originated a nuclear attack. In conjunction with strengthened International Atomic Energy Agency safeguards, states could be required to submit detailed isotopic data on the nuclear materials they produce and to submit to the data's verification. If such states had pure intentions, this would help exclude them from blame were a future terrorist attack to occur; were their motives more suspect, this would provide the world a hedge against their future breakout. So far, states have been loath to take such actions, as they could require compromising sensitive military and commercial data. But the tradeoffs in confronting terrorism—in particular, in the immediate aftermath of an attack—might prompt many to reconsider.

With possession of nuclear weapons comes the responsibility for their control.

The Problem of Intent

The physical identification of bombs with their builders still leaves open the question of intent. Imagine that a bomb made of North Korean plutonium were detonated in Washington:

Would it not be essential, some ask, that we know whether the plutonium had been provided to terrorists intentionally, rather than stolen against the regime's wishes? In fact, it should not matter. Instead, in deciding whether it would be appropriate to retaliate for an attack, we must ask two questions: Is it morally acceptable to retaliate? And is it strategically wise?

Insofar as deterrence itself is morally acceptable (a controversial proposition in some circles, but one at least tacitly accepted in the strategies of all eight nuclear powers), the threat and act of retaliation against an enemy for leaking nuclear materials, whether intentional or otherwise, are moral too. With possession of nuclear weapons comes the responsibility for their control. If a state is unwilling to accept responsibility for the impact of any weapons it builds, it can choose not to build them. By foregoing that choice, it should be understood that the state takes responsibility for any impact the weapons have. To see that such a proposition is widely accepted, one need look no further than the Cold War, where deterrent threats made little or no distinction between intentional and accidental launches of Soviet or U.S. missiles.

The strategic wisdom of retaliation under ambiguous circumstances is another matter entirely. Against an attack originating from North Korea or Iran, whether intentional or not, there would be little for the United States to lose were it to retaliate. Since the result of the retaliation would likely be regime change, it would be effective in removing the nuclear threat. Ideally, that prospect would induce both regimes not only to refrain from exporting nuclear materials but also to secure their stockpiles.

Deciding on a Response

In contrast, if an attack were to originate from loose Russian material, military retaliation would be unwise. It is currently inconceivable that such an attack would be intentional on Russia's part, as Russia is not an enemy; moreover, retaliation would do little to prevent further leakage of Russian material and indeed might provoke Russian retaliation in kind. The precedent for such an approach is also found in the changed U.S. attitude toward accidental missile launch since the Cold War. Does anyone believe that it would be strategically wise for the United States to retaliate militarily against an (improbable) accidental launch of a Russian missile?

Perhaps the toughest case is Pakistan, currently an ally in the war on terrorism. Few U.S. policymakers are confident that Pakistan's nuclear arsenal is entirely secure, making weapons theft by terrorists a distinct possibility. At the same time, many doubt the sincerity of Pakistan's cooperation with the United States, and given its past sales of nuclear equipment to North Korea, Iran, and Libya, there would likely be doubts as to whether nuclear material leaked from Pakistan was proliferated intentionally or was stolen. U.S. policy toward Pakistan on this question will likely depend on how the broader U.S.-Pakistani relationship evolves. President Bush's national security team needs to debate now how it would respond to a leak of Pakistani nuclear material. If it concludes that it will hold the Pakistani regime responsible for any nuclear leaks, it should communicate its decisions clearly, though quietly, to the Pakistani leadership. At the same time, it should offer to help Pakistan secure its arsenal against theft.

Preventing Terrorist Attacks

[In 2003], a National Research Council panel, in addressing the threat of nuclear terrorism, reported that "the technology for developing the needed attribution capability exists but has to be assembled." It noted that an effort to complete that work is under way in the Pentagon's Defense Threat Reduction Agency, but that it is not expected to be complete for several years. If attribution is construed merely as something useful after an attack, perhaps to provide evidence in prosecuting the offenders, it makes sense for it to take a back seat to urgent efforts such as securing ports and improving surveillance. Attribution, however, has the potential to be far more powerful. Coupled with the right threats, it can prevent terrorist attacks in the first place. The scientific effort must be accelerated, and declaratory policy must be modified to match.

CHAPTER

Was Iraq a Weapons of Mass Destruction Threat?

Chapter Preface

The United Nations (UN) Security Council passed resolution 986 on April 14, 1995, creating the UN oil-for-food program (OFFP). The resolution allowed Iraq to export oil through legitimate oil traders in exchange for humanitarian relief meant for ordinary Iraqis suffering under the economic sanctions that had been imposed by the UN at the end of the Gulf War in 1992. The Security Council had originally enacted economic sanctions to punish Saddam Hussein for the Iraqi invasion of Kuwait, which began the Gulf War in 1991; to prevent him from developing weapons of mass destruction; and to completely disarm Iraq. The UN resolution was meant to stay in place until UN weapons inspectors could verify that Iraq was disarmed. The United States, one of the permanent members of the Security Council, imposed a stricter standard. The U.S. Congress passed the Iraq Liberation Act in 1998, stating that a regime change in Iraq was the United States' ultimate goal.

Under the OFFP, Iraq was supposed to sell oil to legitimate oil brokers and receive a comparable value in food and medicine, which should have been distributed to its citizens. Instead, the Iraqi government created a separate, undisclosed (except to the participants) program whereby any persons or businesses favored by the Iraqi government were given oil vouchers in exchange for providing Iraq with cash payments or items banned by the UN sanctions. The voucher recipients traded the vouchers for oil, receiving a commission on each barrel sold. The *Times* of London estimated that Russian and French companies received over $11 billion worth of business from the OFFP between 1996 and 2003. The OFFP executive director, Benon Sevan, received vouchers totaling 11.5 million barrels of oil, which potentially could have yielded a profit between $575,000 and $3.5 million, depending on the commission rate. Kojo Annan, the son of UN secretary-general Kofi Annan, was also involved. He worked for Cotecna, S.A., a French company that was implicated in the kickback scheme. The OFFP scandal became a major embarrassment for the United Nations.

Kofi Annan named former U.S. federal reserve chairman, Paul Volker, to head an investigation into the oil-for-food program in April 2004. The independent commission released its final report on September 7, 2005. The report notes that the OFFP achieved its two main objectives: "depriving Saddam Hussein of WMDs and maintaining minimal standards of nutrition and health in the face of potential crisis." The report, though, harshly criticized the UN administration of the program.

Critics, however, asked whether Saddam used OFFP cash received in kickbacks to revitalize Iraq's weapons programs. During the 2004 U.S. presidential election campaign, President George W. Bush said: "The Duelfer report (the Iraq survey group seeking to find Iraqi WMD after the 2003 U.S. invasion) showed that Saddam was systematically gaming the system, using the U.N. oil for food program to try to influence countries and companies in an effort to undermine sanctions. He was doing so with the intent of restarting his weapons program once the world looked away."

Whether one believes the OFFP was corrupt or merely incompetent, the UN program remains part of the debate over Iraq's WMD progress. The authors of the viewpoints that follow argue from different perspectives whether Saddam and Iraq were indeed a WMD threat to the world.

Iraq Had Weapons of Mass Destruction

Kenneth R. Timmerman

Kenneth R. Timmerman is a senior writer for Insight on the
News, *a weekly newsmagazine.*

New evidence out of Iraq suggests that the U.S. effort to
track down [deposed Iraqi leader] Saddam Hussein's
missing weapons of mass destruction (WMD) is having better
success than is being reported. Key assertions by the intelligence community that were widely judged in the media and
by critics of President George W. Bush as having been false
are turning out to have been true after all. But this stunning
news has received little attention from the major media, and
the president's critics continue to insist that "no weapons"
have been found.

In virtually every case—chemical, biological, nuclear and
ballistic missiles—the United States has found the weapons
and the programs that the Iraqi dictator successfully concealed
for 12 years from U.N. weapons inspectors.

The Iraq Survey Group (ISG), whose intelligence analysts
are managed by Charles Duelfer, a former State Department
official and deputy chief of the U.N.-led arms-inspection
teams, has found "hundreds of cases of activities that were
prohibited" under U.N. Security Council resolutions, a senior
administration official tells *Insight.* "There is a long list of
charges made by the U.S. that have been confirmed, but none
of this seems to mean anything because the weapons that
were unaccounted for by the United Nations remain unaccounted for."

Both Duelfer and his predecessor, David Kay, reported to
Congress that the evidence they had found on the ground in

Iraq showed Saddam's regime was in "material violation" of U.N. Security Council Resolution 1441, the last of 17 resolutions that promised "serious consequences" if Iraq did not make a complete disclosure of its weapons programs and dismantle them in a verifiable manner. The United States cited Iraq's refusal to comply with these demands as one justification for going to war.

A Clandestine Network

Both Duelfer and Kay found that Iraq had "a clandestine network of laboratories and safe houses with equipment that was suitable to continuing its prohibited chemical- [CW] and biological-weapons [BW] programs," the official said. "They found a prison laboratory where we suspect they tested biological weapons on human subjects. They found equipment for uranium-enrichment centrifuges" whose only plausible use was as part of a clandestine nuclear-weapons program. In all these cases, "Iraqi scientists had been told before the war not to declare their activities to the U.N. inspectors," the official said.

A wide variety of biological-weapons agents were found beneath the sink in the home of a prominent Iraqi [biological weapons] scientist.

But while the president's critics and the media might plausibly hide behind ambiguity and a lack of sensational-looking finds for not reporting some discoveries, in the case of Saddam's ballistic-missile programs they have no excuse for their silence. "Where were the missiles? We found them," another senior administration official told *Insight*.

"Saddam Hussein's prohibited missile programs are as close to a slam dunk as you will ever find for violating United Nations resolutions," the first official said. Both senior administration officials spoke to *Insight* on condition that neither their name nor their agency be identified, but their accounts of what the United States has found in Iraq coincided in every major area.

Forbidden Weapons Found

When former weapons inspector Kay reported to Congress in January [2004] that the United States had found "no stockpiles" of forbidden weapons in Iraq, his conclusions made front-page news. But when he detailed what the ISG had found in testimony before the House Permanent Select Committee on Intelligence [in] October [2003], few took notice. Among Kay's revelations, which officials say have been amplified in subsequent inspections in recent weeks:

- A prison laboratory complex that may have been used for human testing of BW agents and "that Iraqi officials working to prepare the U.N. inspections were explicitly ordered not to declare to the U.N." Why was Saddam interested in testing biological-warfare agents on humans if he didn't have a biological-weapons program?

- "Reference strains" of a wide variety of biological-weapons agents were found beneath the sink in the home of a prominent Iraqi BW scientist. "We thought it was a big deal," a senior administration official said. "But it has been written off [by the press] as a sort of 'starter set.'"

- New research on BW-applicable agents, brucella and Congo-Crimean hemorrhagic fever, and continuing work on ricin and aflatoxin that were not declared to the United Nations. . . .

Planning to Produce New WMD

In testimony before Congress on March 30, [2004,] Duelfer revealed that the ISG had found evidence of a "crash program" to construct new plants capable of making chemical-

and biological-warfare agents. The ISG also found a previously undeclared program to build a "high-speed rail gun," a device apparently designed for testing nuclear-weapons materials. That came in addition to 500 tons of natural uranium stockpiled at Iraq's main declared nuclear site south of Baghdad, which International Atomic Energy Agency spokesman Mark Gwozdecky acknowledged to *Insight* had been intended for "a clandestine nuclear-weapons program."

In taking apart Iraq's clandestine procurement network, Duelfer said his investigators had discovered that "the primary source of illicit financing for this system was oil smuggling conducted through government-to-government protocols negotiated with neighboring countries [and] from kickback payments made on contracts set up through the U.N. oil-for-food program"

[WMD] stockpiles have been found, not all at once . . . but found all the same.

What the president's critics and the media widely have portrayed as the most dramatic failure of the U.S. case against Saddam has been the claimed failure to find "stockpiles" of chemical and biological weapons. But in a June 2003 *Washington Post* op-ed, former chief U.N. weapons inspector Rolf Ekeus called such criticism "a distortion and a trivialization of a major threat to international peace and security."

The October 2002 "National Intelligence Estimate on Iraqi Weapons of Mass Destruction" concluded that Saddam "probably has stocked at least 100 metric tons (MT) and possibly as much as 500 MT of CW agents, much of it added in the last year." That assessment was based, in part, on conclusions contained in the final report from U.N. weapons inspectors in 1999, which highlighted discrepancies in what the Iraqis reported to the United Nations and the amount of precursor chemicals U.N. arms inspectors could document Iraq had imported but for which it no longer could account. Until now, Bush's critics say, no stockpiles of CW agents made with those precursors have been found. The snap conclusion they draw is that the administration "lied" to the American people to create a pretext for invading Iraq.

But what are "stockpiles" of CW agents supposed to look like? Was anyone seriously expecting Saddam to have left behind freshly painted warehouses packed with chemical munitions, all neatly laid out in serried rows, with labels written in English? Or did they think that a captured Saddam would guide U.S. troops to smoking vats full of nerve gas in an abandoned factory? In fact, as recent evidence made public by a former operations officer for the Coalition Provisional Authority's (CPA's) intelligence unit in Iraq shows, some of those stockpiles have been found, not all at once and not all in nice working order but found all the same.

Chemical Weapons Evidence

Douglas Hanson was a U.S. Army cavalry reconnaissance officer for 20 years, and a veteran of Gulf War I [in 1991]. He was an atomic demolitions munitions security officer and a nuclear, biological and chemical defense officer. As a civilian analyst in Iraq [in] summer [2003], he worked for an operations intelligence unit of the CPA in Iraq, and later, with the newly formed Ministry of Science and Technology, which was responsible for finding new, nonlethal employment for Iraqi WMD scientists.

In an interview with *Insight* and in an article he wrote for the online magazine *AmericanThinker.com*, Hanson examines reports from U.S. combat units and public information confirming that many of Iraq's CW stockpiles have indeed been found. Until now, however, journalists have devoted scant attention to this evidence, in part because it contradicts the story line they have been putting forward since the U.S.-led inspections began after the war.

But another reason for the media silence may stem from the seemingly undramatic nature of the "finds" Hanson and others have described. The materials that constitute Saddam's chemical-weapons "stockpiles" look an awful lot like pesticides, which they indeed resemble. "Pesticides are the key elements in the chemical-agent arena," Hanson says. "In fact, the general pesticide chemical formula (organophosphate) is the 'grandfather' of modern-day nerve agents."

'At a very minimum [Iraq was] storing the precursors to restart a chemical-warfare program very quickly.'

The United Nations was fully aware that Saddam had established his chemical-weapons plants under the guise of a permitted civilian chemical-industry infrastructure. Plants inspected in the early 1990s as CW production facilities had been set up to appear as if they were producing pesticides or, [as] in the case of a giant plant near Fallujah, chlorine, which is used to produce mustard gas.

When coalition forces entered Iraq, "huge warehouses and caches of 'commercial and agricultural' chemicals were seized and painstakingly tested by Army and Marine chemical specialists," Hanson writes. "What was surprising was how quickly the ISG refuted the findings of our ground forces and how silent they have been on the significance of these caches."

Caches of "commercial and agricultural" chemicals don't match the expectation of "stockpiles" of chemical weapons. But, in fact, that is precisely what they are. "At a very minimum," Hanson tells *Insight*, "they were storing the precursors to restart a chemical-warfare program very quickly." Kay and Duelfer came to a similar conclusion, telling Congress under oath that Saddam had built new facilities and stockpiled the materials to relaunch production of chemical and biological weapons at a moment's notice.

At Karbala, U.S. troops stumbled upon 55-gallon drums of pesticides at what appeared to be a very large "agricultural supply" area, Hanson says. Some of the drums were stored in a "camouflaged bunker complex" that was shown to reporters with unpleasant results. "More than a dozen soldiers, a Knight-Ridder reporter, a CNN cameraman, and two Iraqi POWs [prisoners of war] came down with symptoms consistent with exposure to a nerve agent," Hanson says. "But later ISG tests resulted in a proclamation of negative, end of story, nothing to see here, etc., and the earlier findings and injuries dissolved into nonexistence. Left unexplained is the small matter of the obvious pains taken to disguise the cache of ostensibly legitimate pesticides. One wonders about the advantage an agricultural-commodities business gains by securing drums of pesticide in camouflaged bunkers 6 feet underground. The 'agricultural site' was also co-located with a military ammunition dump, evidently nothing more than a coincidence in the eyes of the ISG."

More WMD Finds

That wasn't the only significant find by coalition troops of probable CW stockpiles, Hanson believes. Near the northern Iraqi town of Bai'ji, where Saddam had built a chemical-weapons plant known to the United States from nearly 12 years of inspections, elements of the 4th Infantry Division found 55-gallon drums containing a substance identified through mass spectrometry analysis as cyclosarin, a nerve agent. Nearby were surface-to-surface and surface-to-air missiles, gas masks and a mobile laboratory that could have been used to mix chemicals at the site. "Of course, later tests by the experts revealed that these were only the ubiquitous pesticides that everybody was turning up," Hanson says. "It seems Iraqi soldiers were obsessed with keeping ammo dumps insect-free, according to the reading of the evidence now enshrined by the conventional wisdom that 'no WMD stockpiles have been discovered.'"

At Taji, an Iraqi weapons complex as large as the District of Columbia, U.S. combat units discovered more "pesticides" stockpiled in specially built containers, smaller in diameter but much longer than the standard 55-gallon drum. Hanson says he still recalls the military sending digital images of the canisters to his office, where his boss at the Ministry of Science and Technology translated the Arabic-language markings. "They were labeled as pesticides," he says. "Gee, you sure have got a lot of pesticides stored in ammo dumps."

'The Iraqis admitted they had made 3.9 tons of VX,' a powerful nerve gas.

Again, [in] January [2004], Danish forces found 120-millimeter mortar shells filled with a mysterious liquid that initially tested positive for blister agents. But subsequent tests by the United States disputed that finding. "If it wasn't a chemical agent, what was it?" Hanson asks. "More pesticides? Dish-washing detergent? From this old soldier's perspective, I gain nothing from putting a liquid in my mortar rounds unless that stuff will do bad things to the enemy."

The discoveries Hanson describes are not dramatic. And that's the problem: Finding real stockpiles in grubby ammo dumps doesn't fit the image the media and the president's critics carefully have fed to the public of what Iraq's weapons ought to look like.

Missing Nerve Gas

A senior administration official who has gone through the intelligence reporting from Iraq as well as the earlier reports from U.N. arms inspectors refers to another well-documented allegation. "The Iraqis admitted they had made 3.9 tons of VX," a powerful nerve gas, but claimed they had never weaponized it. The U.N. inspectors "felt they had more. But where did it go?" The Iraqis never provided any explanation of what had happened to their VX stockpiles.

What does 3.9 tons of VX look like? "It could fit in one large garage," the official says. Assuming, of course, that Saddam would assemble every bit of VX gas his scientists had produced at a single site, that still amounts to one large garage in an area the size of the state of California.

Senior administration officials stress that the investigation will continue as inspectors comb through millions of pages of documents in Iraq and attempt to interview Iraqi weapons scientists who have been trained all their professional lives to conceal their activities from the outside world.

"The conditions under which the ISG is working are not very conducive," one official said. "But this president wants the truth to come out. This is not an exercise in spinning or censoring."

Iraq Moved Its Weapons of Mass Destruction in Response to the U.S. Invasion

Christopher Hitchens

Christopher Hitchens is a contributing editor to Vanity Fair, *a columnist for* Slate, *and the author of numerous books, including* A Long Short War: The Postponed Liberation of Iraq.

Once again, a major story gets top billing in a mainstream paper—and is printed upside down. "Looting at Weapons Plants Was Systematic, Iraqi Says." This was how the *New York Times* led its front page on Sunday [March 13, 2005]. According to the supporting story, Dr. Sami al-Araji, the deputy minister of industry, says that after the fall of Baghdad in April 2003, "looters systematically dismantled and removed tons of machinery from [deposed Iraqi leader] Saddam Hussein's most important weapons installations, including some with high-precision equipment capable of making parts for nuclear arms."

As printed, the implication of the story was not dissimilar from the Al-Qaqaa [Iraqi munitions depot] disclosures, which featured so much in the closing days of the presidential election [in fall 2004]. In that case, a huge stock of conventional high-explosives had been allowed to go missing and was presumably in the hands of those who were massacring Iraqi civilians and killing coalition troops. At least one comment from the [George W.] Bush campaign [circuit] appeared to blame this negligence on the troops themselves. Followed to one possible conclusion, the implication was clear: The invasion of Iraq had made the world a more dangerous place by randomly scattering all sorts of weaponry, including mass-destruction weaponry, to destinations unknown.

Looting Nuclear Weapons Labs

It was eye-rubbing to read of the scale of this potential new nightmare. There in cold print was the Al Hatteen "munitions production plant that international inspectors called a complete potential nuclear weapons laboratory." And what of the Al Adwan facility, which "produced equipment used for uranium enrichment, necessary to make some kinds of nuclear weapons"? The overall pattern of the plundered sites was summarized thus, by reporters James Glanz and William J. Broad:

> The kinds of machinery at the various sites included equipment that could be used to make missile parts, chemical weapons or centrifuges essential for enriching uranium for atom bombs.

My first question is this: How can it be that, on every page of every other edition for months now, the *New York Times* has been stating categorically that Iraq harbored no weapons of mass destruction? And there can hardly be a comedy-club third-rater or MoveOn.org [a liberal political action group] activist in the entire country who hasn't stated with sarcastic certainty that the whole WMD [weapons of mass destruction] fuss was a way of lying the American people into war. So now what? Maybe we should have taken Saddam's propaganda seriously, when his newspaper proudly described Iraq's physicists as "our nuclear mujahideen [holy warriors]."

Saddam's Iraq was a fairly highly-evolved WMD state.

Post-invasion Plans

My second question is: What's all this about "looting"? The word is used throughout the long report, but here's what it's used to describe. "In four weeks from mid-April to mid-May of 2003 ... teams with flatbed trucks and other heavy equipment moved systematically from site to site. . . . 'The first wave came for the machines,' Dr Araji said. 'The second wave, cables and cranes.'" Perhaps hedging the bet, the *Times* authors at this point refer to "organized looting."

But obviously, what we are reading about is a carefully planned military operation. The participants were not panicked or greedy civilians helping themselves—which is the customary definition of a "looter," especially in wartime. They were mechanized and mobile and under orders, and acting in a concerted fashion. Thus, if the story is factually correct—which we have no reason at all to doubt—then Saddam's Iraq was a fairly highly-evolved WMD state, with a contingency plan for further concealment and distribution of the weaponry in case of attack or discovery.

Before the war began, several of the administration's critics argued that an intervention would be too dangerous, either because Saddam Hussein would actually unleash his arsenal of WMD, or because he would divert it to third parties. That case at least had the merit of being serious (though I would want to argue that a regime capable of doing either thing was a regime that urgently needed to be removed). Since then, however, the scene has dissolved into one long taunt and jeer: "There *were* no WMD in Iraq. Liar, liar, pants on fire."

If Saddam's people could have made such a [WMD] transfer after his fall, then they could have made it much more easily during his reign.

The U.N. inspectors, who are solemnly quoted by Glanz and Broad as having "monitored" the alarming developments at Al Hatteen and elsewhere, don't come out looking too professional, either. If by scanning satellite pictures now they can tell us that potentially thermonuclear stuff is on the loose, how come they couldn't come up with this important data when they were supposedly "on the ground"?

WMD Manipulation

Even in the worst interpretation, it seems unlikely that the material is more dangerous now than it was [at the beginning of the invasion in 2003]. Some of the elements—centrifuges, for example, and chemical mixtures—require stable and controlled conditions for effectiveness. They can't simply be transferred to some kitchen or tent. They are less risky than they were in early 2003, in other words. If they went to a neighboring state, though ... Some chemical vats have apparently turned up on a scrap heap in Jordan, even if this does argue more for a panicky concealment than a plan of transfer. But anyway, this only returns us to the main point: If Saddam's people could have made such a transfer after his fall, then they could have made it much more easily during his reign. (We know, for example, that the Baathists [Saddam's ruling party] were discussing the acquisition of long-range missiles from North Korea as late as March 2003, and at that time, the nuclear Wal-Mart of the A.Q. Khan [Pakistani scientist and businessman who illegally sold nuclear technology worldwide] network was still in business. Iraq would have had plenty to trade in this WMD underworld.)

Supporters of the overdue disarmament and liberation of Iraq, all the same, can't be complacent about this story. It seems flabbergasting that any of these sites were unsecured after the occupation, let alone for so long. Did the CIA yet again lack "human intelligence" as well as every other kind? The Bush administration staked the reputation of the United States on the matter. It won't do to say that "mistakes were made."

Saddam Hussein Was Iraq's Weapon of Mass Destruction

Victor Davis Hanson

Victor Davis Hanson is a senior fellow at the Hoover Institution at Stanford University. He is a nationally syndicated columnist and writes a weekly column for National Review Online. *He is the author of numerous books, including* An Autumn of War *and* Ripples of Battle.

The United States has lost less than 350 American dead in actual combat in Iraq [as of February 2004], deposed the worst tyrant on the planet, and offered the first real hope of a humane government in the recent history of the Middle East—and is being roundly condemned rather than praised for one of the most remarkable occurrences of our age. Yet a careful postbellum anatomy of the recent WMD [weapons of mass destruction] controversy makes the original case for the war stronger rather than weaker.

A Weapon of Mass Destruction

There were four unique factors in the calculus involving [Iraqi leader] Saddam Hussein and his so-called weapons of mass destruction: (1) Saddam Hussein had petrodollars [money from oil] to buy such strategic weapons; (2) He had acquired and stockpiled such arms and used them in war against Iran and in peace against his own people; (3) He had a long history of aggression against the United States—from Gulf War I to trying to assassinate an American president; and (4) His Baathist [Party] police state had a systematic policy of hiding such weapons, from both the United States postwar intelligence gatherers and the U.N. inspectors.

Therefore as long as Saddam Hussein was in power it mattered little what the professed status of his chemical and bio-

Victor Davis Hanson, "Weapons of Mass Hysteria," *National Review Online*, February 6, 2004. Reproduced by permission.

logical arsenal was at any particular time, since our only certain knowledge was that he had a proven desire and ability to purchase, re-create, and use them on any given day—*and that day would be mostly unknown to everyone outside of Iraq.* He may have had thousands of tons of weapons in 1980, hundreds of tons in 1990, and tens of tons in 1995, almost zero in 2003—and yet once again perhaps hundreds in 2005 and thousands again in 2010. Thus the cliché that Saddam Hussein himself was the weapon of mass destruction was in fact entirely accurate.

After September 11 it was no longer tolerable to allow Middle East dictators to continue as rogue states.

Throughout this war there has been consistently fuzzy nomenclature that reflects mistaken logic: WMDs are supposedly the problem, rather than the tyrannical regimes that stockpile them—as if [British prime minister] Tony Blair's nuclear arsenal threatens world peace; we are warring against the method of "terror" rather than states that promote or allow it—as if the Cold War was a struggle against SAM-6's [Soviet antiballistic missiles] or KGB-like [Soviet intelligence agency] tactics; [The terrorist attacks of] September 11 [2001] had nothing to do with the Iraqi war, as if after 3,000 Americans were butchered through unconventional and terrorist tactics the margin of tolerance against Middle East tyrannical regimes that seek the weapons of such a trade does not diminish radically.

The Need for Action

The threat of WMDs may have been the centerpiece of the administration's arguments to go to war, but for most of us, there were plenty of other—and far more important—reasons for prompt action now.

Let us for the *nth* time recite them: Saddam had broken the 1991 armistice agreements and after September 11 it was no longer tolerable to allow Middle East dictators to continue as rogue states and virtual belligerents. Two-thirds of Iraqi airspace were de facto controlled by the United States—ultimately an unsustainable commitment requiring over a decade of daily vigilance, billions of dollars, and hundreds of thousands of sorties to prevent further genocide. He had defied U.N. resolutions; and he had expelled inspectors, demanding either enforcement or appeasement and subsequent humiliation of the international community.

A number of accounts had cited relationships between al Qaeda and Baathist intelligence.

It really was an intolerable situation that in perpetuity thousands of Kurds [an ethnic minority in Iraq] and Shiites [minority Muslim sect] were doomed on any given week that American and British planes might have been grounded. Saddam had a history of war against Kuwait, Saudi Arabia, Israel, Iran, and the United States, destroyed the ecology of the Mesopotamian wetlands, gassed his own people, and relented in his massacres only to the degree that the United States monitored him constantly. Should we continue with the shameful litany?

Well, in addition, in northern Iraq al Qaedists [terrorists responsible for the September 11 attacks] were battling the Kurds. Old-line terrorists like Abu Abbas and Abu Nidal were at home in Baghdad. Husseinite bounties subsidized suicide-murdering in Israel. A number of accounts had cited relationships between al Qaeda and Baathist intelligence. Iraq, in fact, was already at a critical mass. Faced with a brutal, unending U.N. embargo and the loss of its airspace, it was descending into a badland like Afghanistan. The amorality is not that we took him out, but that after 1991 we waited about 100,000 corpses too long.

"Intelligence" Is Rarely Intelligent

It is regrettable that two successive administrations apparently (inasmuch as the complete truth really does await translations of the Iraqi archives, a complete inquiry of former Baathists, and assurances from Syria) have had no accurate idea of the extent, or lack thereof, of the Iraqi WMD arsenal. But incomplete or faulty intelligence—both hysterical overreactions or laxity and naiveté—is not rare when nations go to war.

The emphasis on weapons of mass destruction in Iraq, . . . [has] had a powerful effect on such arsenals far beyond Baghdad.

We were fooled by Japan in 1941 [at Pearl Harbor] and had no idea that its enormous fleet was a few hundred miles off Hawaii. The Soviet absorption of Eastern Europe caught utopians off guard in 1945–6. Everyone underestimated [Chinese Communist leader] Mao's resilience. [U.S. general Douglas] MacArthur's "infiltrators" across the Yalu River [the boundary between North and South Korea] turned out to be several Chinese armies. We know only now that the Soviets cheated on several major arms agreements—and had WMD arsenals far beyond what was disclosed. Its nuclear accidents and WMD catastrophes are still clouded in mysteries. Remember the Missile Gap of the 1960 [presidential] election that helped to elect John Kennedy? Yet Cuba, we now learn, had more ready nukes than even [U.S. Air Force general] Curtis LeMay imagined. The British surely had no warning about the Falklands invasion [1982 Argentine attack on British islands off South America]. An American ambassador gave the wrong message to Saddam Hussein in summer 1990, precisely because the CIA had no clue that Saddam Hussein was gearing up to invade Kuwait. Libya and Iran were further along with their nuclear programs than the CIA dared to imagine. Ditto North Korea. Who knew that Pakistan has been running a nuclear clearinghouse? The point is not to excuse faulty intelligence, but rather to understand that knowing exactly what the enemy is up to is difficult and yet almost never acknowledged to be so.

The Wages of Bluffing

If present stockpiles of WMDs are discovered not to have been present in Iraq in spring 2003 or to have been transported to Syria, it is probably because of deception inside Iraq itself. Either Iraqi weapons procurers and scientists may have misled an unhinged Saddam Hussein or Saddam knew he had no arsenal and yet deliberately misled the U.N. In other words, if the world decides that such a monster cannot have such weapons (as the U.N., in fact, did in several resolutions), and such a monster chooses for whatever bizarre reasons to avoid disclosing information about them, then either one acts on logical inferences or does not—and thus accepts the wages of such defiance.

I am sorry that the United States has established a hair-trigger reputation in matters of deadly agents of mass destruction—but apparently other rogue nations now believe that the burden of proof is no longer on us to establish that they have them, but rather on them to ensure the world that they do not. And that is not necessarily a bad thing if we ponder that the lives of thousands may hang in the balance.

WMD Deterrence

So it turns out that the emphasis on weapons of mass destruction in Iraq, and the subsequent effort to take out Saddam Hussein have had a powerful effect on such arsenals far beyond Baghdad. Without the removal of the Baathists, Libya would never have confessed to its nuclear roguery. Without the recent [Iraq] war, Iran would never have *professed* a desire to follow international protocols. Without the recent conflict, Pakistan would never have investigated its own outlaw scientists.

Whether we like it or not, the precedent that the United Sates might act decisively against regimes that were both suspected of pursuing WMD acquisition and doing nothing to allay those fears, has had a powerful prophylactic effect in the neighborhood. Only in this Orwellian [characterized by double-talk] election year [2004], would candidates for the presidency decry that the war had nothing to do with the dilemma of WMDs—even as Libya, Iran, and Pakistan by their very actions apparently disagreed.

The work of a psychopath and his sons . . . have now been put permanently out of the business of mass death.

Cost-Benefit Analysis

A decade-long U.N. trade embargo, coupled with occasional U.S. [air] strikes (the 1999 Desert Fox operation [bombings of Iraqi weapons facilities] may have killed 4,000 Iraqis) probably led to as much damage and death as the recent war—but without either freeing the Iraqi people or finally ascertaining the exact nature of Saddam's chemical, biological, and nuclear arsenal. Once Saddam Hussein took Iraq down the path of tyranny, invasion, and WMD acquisition, then it was not a question of stopping him without losses, but simply finding the most economical way to rid the world of his regime at the least cost in lives. When reckoned over a 30-year era, the recent war will have seemed humane in comparison to what transpired between 1975 and 2003.

Again, I am sorry that [U.S. weapons inspector] David Kay's preliminary findings suggest an intelligence lapse; but that sorrow is mitigated by the recognition that there are tens of thousands of rotting skulls in the deserts of Iraq—the work of a psychopath and his sons, who, thanks to the belated efforts of the United States, have now been put permanently out of the business of mass death.

WMD Paranoia

While conventional arsenals kill far more than [do] chemical or biological weapons, the latter hold a particular horror for us all given the stealthy nature of microbes and gas, and their theoretical ability to kill us en masse without the scream of an artillery shell or burp of a machine gun. Illogical perhaps, but true nonetheless is our paranoia about these horrific weapons. My grandfather who was mustard gassed in the [battle for the] Argonne [Forest during World War I] coughed out horrific tales of yellow clouds; rarely [of] artillery bursts that killed most of his friends. The Chinese demand reparations from Japan over the brutality of Unit 731 [Japanese military unit that conducted biological warfare experiments on Chinese civilians during World War II] in a way they do not even concerning the Rape of Nanking [Chinese city pillaged by Japanese troops during World War II]. A few grains of Ricin [a toxic agent] empty the [U.S.] Capitol in a way a random artillery shell or abandoned M-16 would not.

Unconventional weapons, in other words, by their very nature of stealth, horrific death, and the failure of conventional military deterrence scare people—especially in the present context of asymmetrical warfare where rogue states and terrorist cells seek them precisely to nullify Western military advantage. This is not to excuse WMD paranoia, but only to suggest, for example, that [then-secretary of state] Colin Powell's excursus to the U.N. might in retrospect been inaccurate in all its details, but nevertheless a well-meaning effort to ensure the United States did not experience something like the cloud in Kurdistan—or unconventional and unpredictable acts analogous to September 11.

Iraq Did Not Possess Weapons of Mass Destruction

World Socialist Web Site Editorial Board

The World Socialist Web Site examines political and social issues from a socialist perspective. Its editorial board oversees its publications.

The report released October 6 [2004] by Charles Duelfer, head of the Iraq Survey Group (ISG), is an indictment not merely of a president or an administration, but of an entire ruling elite. The report confirms that the claims about Iraq's supposed weapons of mass destruction, advanced by three US administrations, Democratic and Republican, and parroted uncritically by the American media, were outright lies.

The Iraqi government was telling the truth about its alleged stockpiles of WMD. UN inspectors Mohammed ElBaradei and Hans Blix were telling the truth about the lack of any evidence of WMD stockpiles or nuclear weapons activity. Former [UN] weapons inspector Scott Ritter was telling the truth when he said Iraq had long before dismantled its WMD capacity.

The hundreds of millions of people around the world who saw through the lies of the American government and demonstrated in dozens of countries against the US invasion were right. It is US imperialism that stands condemned for taking a page from the book of [Nazi propaganda minister Joseph] Goebbels and using the technique of the "Big Lie" to carry out a criminal conspiracy.

World Socialist Web Site Editorial Board, "Iraq WMD Report Proves Bush, Democrats Lied to Justify Iraq War," October 8, 2004. Reproduced by permission.

Inspections Found No WMD

The Duelfer report found that Iraq's chemical and biological weapons were destroyed in 1991 and never reconstituted. The country did not possess a nuclear weapons program and was doing nothing to develop either the materials or the production techniques required to build nuclear weapons. On the contrary, under the impact of a devastating US-backed economic blockade—which caused the deaths of an estimated one million Iraqis, half of them children, for lack of food and medical supplies—the country's ability to sustain any sort of military establishment steadily deteriorated.

Trailers that US officials claimed were mobile biological weapons laboratories were actually being used to make hydrogen for weather balloons.

The Iraq Survey Group mobilized more than 1,200 inspectors under the direction of the CIA and searched the country for 15 months following the US invasion. It found none of the stockpiles, weapons factories, secret laboratories or other facilities claimed by the [George W.] Bush administration. The evidence gathered by the ISG disproved all of the most-publicized declarations by officials of the White House, Pentagon, State Department and CIA during the runup to the invasion of Iraq.

- There was no active Iraqi nuclear weapons program. According to Duelfer, the ISG investigation "uncovered no indication that Iraq had resumed fissile material or nuclear weapons research and development activities since 1991."

- Iraq imported aluminum tubes to use in producing small military rockets, as Iraqi officials had said, not as parts for centrifuges to enrich uranium.

- Iraq did not try to buy uranium overseas after 1991, and even rejected an offer of uranium from an African businessman, citing UN sanctions.

- The trailers that US officials claimed were mobile biological weapons laboratories were actually being used to make hydrogen for weather balloons, as the Iraqis said.

- There was no "red line" south of Baghdad, where Iraqi troops armed with chemical weapons were supposed to unleash WMD on invading US troops.

Duelfer, who spent six years as the deputy head of the UN weapons inspectors in Iraq, was selected to head the ISG by CIA Director George Tenet, and enjoyed the warmest relations with the Bush White House. Before taking the ISG post, he had said he was convinced that there was a connection between Iraq and the September 11 [2001,] terrorist attacks. But when he appeared before the Senate Armed Services Committee to present his report [on October 6, 2004], he told the panel, "We were almost all wrong" on Iraq.

Iraq's unconventional weapons programs were virtually abandoned after the 1991 Persian Gulf War.

Bush administration officials have combed the ISG report for anything they could use to justify their claims that [Saddam] Hussein's Iraq represented a threat to US national security. They have cited claims that Hussein retained the "capability and the intention" to possess dangerous weapons, as Deputy Secretary of State Richard Armitage put it. This is so much clutching at straws.

While Duelfer speculated that Hussein intended to develop chemical, biological and nuclear weapons in the event UN sanctions were lifted, he admitted that the ISG had found no actual plans or other evidence to substantiate such conjectures. As for the "capability," this only means that Iraq, like any other country with even a modest industrial base, had scientists and engineers who could have produced such weapons if given the resources and facilities to do so.

The War Against Iraq Was Based on WMD Lies

Perhaps the most important finding of the ISG is that Iraq's unconventional weapons programs were virtually abandoned after the 1991 Persian Gulf War. The Hussein regime originally developed chemical weapons for use in the Iran-Iraq War of 1980–88, which Hussein initiated, at US instigation, and in which he functioned as a virtual US agent, attacking the Islamic fundamentalist regime that had overthrown the Shah, the principal US ally in the region.

US officials stepped up military, intelligence and diplomatic aid to Iraq even after the widespread use of chemical weapons against Iranian troops had been confirmed. Donald Rumsfeld, now secretary of defense, served as a special envoy to Iraq in 1983–84, visiting Baghdad twice to reassure Hussein of continued support from the [Ronald] Reagan administration.

In 1991, after US troops drove the Iraqi forces out of Kuwait, killing tens of thousands of virtually defenseless conscripts, Hussein accepted a strict regime of UN weapons inspection which quickly dismantled his chemical weapons facilities, as well as research programs on nuclear and biological weapons. The last research facility was destroyed in 1996, according to the ISG report.

Yet throughout the 1990s, Iraq's alleged possession of weapons of mass destruction and its supposed refusal to cooperate with UN weapons inspectors were cited over and over by US officials as the basis for the continued economic strangulation of the country. The first Bush administration [of George H.W. Bush] began this long-running fraud; the [Bill] Clinton administration continued it for eight years (1993–

2001); the second Bush administration [of George W.] took the matter to its conclusion, with the invasion and conquest of Iraq.

The End of the Soviet Union and WMD Fraud

It is not an accident that the WMD fraud began in 1991; that was the year of the collapse of the Soviet Union. Even during the Persian Gulf War, which ended in February 1991, the first Bush administration was constrained from marching on Baghdad and seizing full control of the oil-rich country by the existence of the USSR, a potent military adversary with long-standing ties to the [Iraq's] Ba'athist [Party] regime.

With the end of the USSR in December 1991, US imperialism no longer feared military retaliation or had to reckon with Soviet aid to Iraq. A consensus rapidly developed within the American ruling elite to seize control of the country's oil wealth and establish an American military and political foothold in the crucial region of the Middle East.

There were different shades of opinion over how best to accomplish this. The first Bush administration was wary of a US ground war and military occupation in the Middle East. It believed that the impact of military defeat, sanctions and US covert and overt actions would result in the fall of Saddam Hussein, and enable the US to install a more pliant regime. In the meantime, it backed Hussein against the [minority] Kurdish and Shi'ite uprisings, fearing these would lead to an Iraq aligned with Iran.

When the expected military coup against Saddam failed to materialize, factions that were dissatisfied with the results of the first [gulf] war [in 1991] and determined to push for a US military invasion and occupation of Iraq stepped up their activities. In 1992, Paul Wolfowitz, working at the direction of Richard Cheney, then the secretary of defense [under George

H.W. Bush], drew up the first plans for long-term US military intervention in the Middle East.

As the sanctions [against Iraq] began to unravel, . . . the US ruling elite increasingly turned towards war as the desirable option.

The Neo-conservatives Forge a WMD War

This document was the first draft of the program advocated by neo-conservatives in groups such as the Project for a New American Century, who called for worldwide American hegemony and a policy of "regime change" against any country that they deemed an obstacle to US foreign policy.

[President Bill] Clinton sought to pursue an intensified version of the strategy of the first Bush administration. His administration carried out repeated cruise missile strikes and two brief but bloody bombing campaigns, organized provocations by the UN inspectors, maintained the sanctions and the "no-fly" zones, and infiltrated CIA agents among the UN inspectors in order to plan the assassination of Saddam Hussein. Clinton also authorized several abortive coup attempts, as well as overt CIA terrorist actions, including those carried out in the mid-1990s by Ayad Allawi, now the US-appointed interim prime minister [of Iraq]. Clinton also signed the Iraq Liberation Act, making "regime change" the official policy of the United States.

As the sanctions began to unravel, and US rivals such as France and Russia more aggressively pursued their political and oil interests in Iraq, the US ruling elite increasingly turned towards war as the desirable option. With the installation of the [George W.] Bush administration, inaugurated in January 2001, the proponents of invasion and occupation came to power. Their plans for an invasion of Iraq were well under way when [the terrorist attacks of] 9/11 occurred—under mysterious and still unexplained circumstances—and provided a pretext that they eagerly seized on to prepare the execution of their plans.

From the beginning, the US has used the WMD issue as a cover for its predatory aims. It was a convenient red herring, which was used to justify provocations and military strikes and provide an all-purpose pretext for destroying the country and asserting US domination. It also served to frighten and disorient the public, and condition it to accede to a "preemptive" war against Iraq.

Iraq Never Trained al Qaeda to Use Weapons of Mass Destruction

Robert Scheer

Robert Scheer is a former columnist for the Los Angeles Times *and the author of* With Enough Shovels: Reagan, Bush and Nuclear War.

Who in the White House knew about DITSUM No. 044-02 and when did they know it?

That's the newly declassified smoking-gun document, originally prepared by the Defense Intelligence Agency [DIA] in February 2002 but ignored by President [George W.] Bush. Its declassification [on November 5, 2005,] blows another huge hole in Bush's claim that he was acting on the best intelligence available when he pitched the invasion of Iraq as a way to prevent an Al Qaeda terror attack using weapons of mass destruction.

The report demolished the credibility of the key Al Qaeda informant the administration relied on to make its claim that a working alliance existed between [Iraqi leader] Saddam Hussein and [Al Qaeda leader] Osama bin Laden. It was circulated widely within the U.S. government a full eight months before Bush used the prisoner's lies to argue for an invasion of Iraq because "we've learned that Iraq has trained Al Qaeda members in bomb making and poisons and deadly gases."

Intentionally Misleading

Al Qaeda senior military trainer Ibn al-Shaykh al-Libi—a Libyan captured in Pakistan in 2001—was probably "intentionally misleading the debriefers," the DIA report concluded in one of two paragraphs finally declassified at the request of Sen. Carl Levin (D-Mich.) and released by his office over the weekend. The report also said: "Ibn al-Shaykh has been undergoing debriefs for several weeks and may be describing scenarios to the debriefers that he knows will retain their interest."

He got that right. Folks in the highest places were very interested in claims along the lines Libi was peddling, even though they went against both logic and the preponderance of intelligence gathered to that point about possible collaboration between two enemies of the U.S. that were fundamentally at odds with each other. Al Qaeda was able to create a base in Iraq only after the U.S. overthrow of Hussein, not before. "Saddam's regime is intensely secular and is wary of Islamic revolutionary movements," accurately noted the DIA.

Yet Bush used the informant's already discredited tall tale in his key Oct. 7, 2002, speech just before the Senate voted on whether to authorize the use of force in Iraq and again in two speeches in February [2003], just ahead of the invasion.

The exotic intelligence factoids Bush's researchers culled from raw intelligence . . . have been exposed as previously known frauds.

Leading up to the war, Secretary of State Colin Powell tried to sell it to the United Nations, while Vice President Dick Cheney, national security advisor Condoleezza Rice, White House spokesman Ari Fleischer and Undersecretary of Defense Douglas Feith repeated it breathlessly for homeland audiences. The con worked, and Americans came to believe the lie that Hussein was associated with the Sept. 11 hijackers.

A List of False Evidence

Even CIA Director George Tenet publicly fell into line, ignoring his own agency's dissent that Libi would not have been in a position to know what he said he knew. In fact, Libi, according to the DIA, could not name any Iraqis involved, any chemical or biological material used or where the training allegedly occurred. In January 2004, the prisoner recanted his story, and the next month the CIA withdrew all intelligence reports based on his false information.

The Bush White House systematically ignored the best available intelligence from U.S. agencies.

One by one, the exotic intelligence factoids Bush's researchers culled from raw intelligence data files to publicly bolster their claim of imminent threat—the yellowcake uranium [used to make nuclear weapons] from Niger, the aluminum tubes for processing uranium, the Prague meeting with Mohamed Atta [leader of the September 11, 2001, suicide hijackers], the discredited Iraqi informants "Curveball [an informant who was a chief source of prewar U.S. intelligence about Iraqi biological weapons]" and Ahmad Chalabi [now deputy prime minister in Iraq and former interim oil minister]—have been exposed as previously known frauds.

When it came to selling an invasion of Iraq it had wanted to launch before 9/11, the Bush White House systematically ignored the best available intelligence from U.S. agencies or any other reliable source.

Exploiting Horror and Fear

It should be remembered that while Bush and his gang were successfully scaring the wits out of us about the alleged Iraq-Al Qaeda alliance, U.N. weapons inspectors were on the ground in Iraq. Weapons inspectors Hans Blix and 2005 Nobel Peace Prize winner Mohamed ElBaradei promised they could finish scouring the country if given a few more months. But instead, they were abruptly chased out by an invasion necessitated by what the president told us was a "unique and urgent threat."

Bush exploited the worldwide horror felt over the 9/11 attacks to justify the Iraq invasion. His outrageous claim, repeated over and over before and after he dragged the nation into an unnecessary war, was never supported by a single piece of credible evidence. The Bush defense of what is arguably the biggest lie ever put over on the American people is that everyone had gotten the intelligence wrong. Not so at the highest level of U.S. intelligence, as DITSUM No. 044-02 so clearly shows. How could the president not have known?

The U.S. Government Misled the Public About Iraq's Nuclear Threat

Jason Leopold

Jason Leopold is a freelance journalist and former Los Angeles bureau chief for Dow Jones Newswires.

Six months before the United States was dead-set on invading Iraq to rid the country of its alleged weapons of mass destruction, experts in the field of nuclear science warned officials in the [George W.] Bush administration that intelligence reports showing Iraq was stockpiling chemical and biological weapons was unreliable and that the country did not pose an imminent threat to its neighbors in the Middle East or the U.S.

But the dissenters were told to keep quiet by high-level administration officials in the White House because the Bush administration had already decided that military force would be used to overthrow the regime of Iraq's President Saddam Hussein, interviews and documents have revealed.

The most vocal opponent to intelligence information supplied by the CIA to the hawks in the Bush administration about the so-called Iraqi threat to national security was David Albright, a former United Nations weapons inspector and the president and founder of the Institute for Science and International Security [ISIS], a Washington, D.C. based group that gathers information for the public and the White House on nuclear weapons programs.

Playing the Nuclear Card

With the likelihood of finding WMD in Iraq becoming increasingly remote, new information, such as documents and

Jason Leopold, "White House Silenced Experts Who Questioned Iraq Intel Six Months Before War," AntiWar.com, June 12, 2003. Reprinted with permission.

135

interviews provided by Albright and other weapons experts, prove that the White House did not suffer so much from an intelligence failure on Iraq's WMD [weapons of mass destruction], but instead shows how the Bush administration embellished reams of intelligence and relied on murky intelligence in order to get Congress and the public to back the war. That may explain why it is becoming so difficult to find WMD: Because it's entirely likely that the weapons don't exist.

"A critical question is whether the Bush Administration has deliberately misled the public and other governments in playing a 'nuclear card' that it knew would strengthen public support for war," Albright said in a March 10 [2003] assessment of the CIA's intelligence, which is posted on the ISIS website.

John Dean, the former counsel to President Richard Nixon, wrote in a column [in June 2003] that if President Bush misled the public in building a case for war in Iraq, a case for impeachment could be made.

"Presidential statements, particularly on matters of national security, are held to an expectation of the highest standard of truthfulness," Dean wrote. "A president cannot stretch, twist or distort facts and get away with it. President Lyndon Johnson's distortions of the truth about Vietnam forced him to stand down from reelection. President Richard Nixon's false statements about Watergate forced his resignation."

[Bush] administration officials were presenting 'embellishments' on information long known about Iraq.

Embellishing Iraqi Capabilities

In September [2002], *USA Today* reported that "the Bush administration is expanding on and in some cases contradicting U.S. intelligence reports in making the case for an invasion of Iraq, interviews with administration and intelligence officials indicate."

"Administration officials accuse Iraq of having ties to al-Qaeda terrorists and of amassing weapons of mass destruction despite uncertain and sometimes contrary intelligence on these issues, according to officials," the paper reported. "In some cases, top administration officials disagree outright with what the CIA and other intelligence agencies report. For example, they repeat accounts of al-Qaeda members seeking refuge in Iraq and of terrorist operatives meeting with Iraqi intelligence officials, even though U.S. intelligence reports raise doubts about such links. On Iraqi weapons programs, administration officials draw the most pessimistic conclusions from ambiguous evidence."

In secret intelligence briefings [in] September [2002] on the Iraqi threat, House Minority Whip Nancy Pelosi, D-Calif., said administration officials were presenting "embellishments" on information long known about Iraq.

Many officials in the intelligence community knew [that found aluminum] tubes weren't meant to build a nuclear weapon.

A senior Bush administration official conceded privately that there are large gaps in U.S. knowledge about Iraqi weapons programs, *USA Today* reported.

Building a Fake Nuke

The concerns jibe with warnings about the CIA's intelligence information which Albright first raised [in] September [2002], when the agency zeroed in on high-strength aluminum tubes Iraq was trying to obtain as evidence of the country's active near-complete nuclear weapons program.

The case of the aluminum tubes is significant because President Bush identified it during a speech [in 2002] as evidence of Iraq's nuclear weapons program and used it to rally the public and several U.N. countries in supporting the war.

But Albright said many officials in the intelligence community knew the tubes weren't meant to build a nuclear weapon.

"The CIA has concluded that these tubes were specifically manufactured for use in gas centrifuges to enrich uranium," Albright said. "Many in the expert community both inside and outside government, however, do not agree with this conclusion. The vast majority of gas centrifuge experts in this country and abroad who are knowledgeable about this case reject the CIA's case and do not believe that the tubes are specifically designed for gas centrifuges. In addition, International Atomic Energy Agency inspectors have consistently expressed skepticism that the tubes are for centrifuges."

"After months of investigation, the administration has failed to prove its claim that the tubes are intended for use in an Iraqi gas centrifuge program," Albright added. "Despite being presented with evidence countering this claim, the administration persists in making misleading comments about the significance of the tubes."

Albright said he tried to voice his concerns about the intelligence information to White House officials [in 2002], but was rebuffed and told to keep quiet.

The Department of Energy . . . rejected the CIA's intelligence analysis.

Silencing Government Scientists

"I first learned of this case a year and a half ago when I was asked for information about past Iraqi procurements. My reaction at the time was that the disagreement reflected the typical in-fighting between US experts that often afflicts the intelligence community. I was frankly surprised when the administration latched onto one side of this debate in September 2002. I was told that this dispute had not been mediated by a competent, impartial technical committee, as it should have been, according to accepted practice," Albright said. "I became dismayed when a knowledgeable government scientist told me that the administration could say anything it wanted about the tubes while government scientists who disagreed were expected to remain quiet."

Albright said the Department of Energy, which analyzed the intelligence information on the aluminum tubes and rejected the CIA's intelligence analysis, is the only government agency in the U.S. that can provide expert opinions on gas centrifuges (what the CIA alleged the tubes were being used for) and nuclear weapons programs.

"For over a year and a half, an analyst at the CIA has been pushing the aluminum tube story, despite consistent disagreement by a wide range of experts in the United States and abroad," Albright said. "His opinion, however, obtained traction in the summer of 2002 with senior members of the Bush Administration, including the President. The administration was forced to admit publicly that dissenters exist, particularly at the Department of Energy and its national laboratories."

Attacking the Dissenters

But Albright said the White House launched an attack against experts who spoke critically of the intelligence.

Former scientists who worked on Iraq's nuclear weapons program . . . also disputed the CIA's intelligence.

"Administration officials try to minimize the number and significance of the dissenters or unfairly attack them," Albright said. "For example, when Secretary [of State Colin] Powell mentioned the dissent in his [UN] Security Council speech, he said: 'Other experts, and the Iraqis themselves, argue that they are really to produce the rocket bodies for a conventional weapon, a multiple rocket launcher.' Not surprisingly, an effort by those at the Energy Department to change Powell's comments before his appearance was rebuffed by the administration."

Moreover, former scientists who worked on Iraq's nuclear weapons program and escaped the country also disputed the CIA's intelligence of the country's existing nuclear weapons program, saying it ended in 1991 after the first Gulf War. However, some Iraq scientists who supplied the Pentagon with information claim that Iraq's nuclear weapons program continues, but none of these Iraqis have any direct knowledge of any current banned nuclear programs. They appear to all carry political baggage and biases about going to war or overthrowing Saddam Hussein, and these biases seem to drive their judgments about nuclear issues, rendering their statements about current Iraqi nuclear activities suspect, according to Albright, who said he was privy to much of the information being supplied to the Bush administration and the CIA.

[At] a classified briefing on Iraq in late 2002 . . . there was laughter in the room when the uranium evidence was presented.

Another example of disputed intelligence used by the Bush administration to build its case for war is Iraq's attempts to obtain uranium from Niger as evidence of another secret nuclear weapons program. Bush, in his State of the Union Speech in January [2003], used this information as an example of a "smoking gun" and the imminent threat Iraq posed to the U.S. But the information has since been widely discounted.

"One person who heard a classified briefing on Iraq in late 2002 said that there was laughter in the room when the uranium evidence was presented," Albright said. "One of (the) most dramatic findings, revealed on March 7, [2003,] was that the documents which form the basis for the reports of recent uranium transactions between Niger and Iraq are not authentic."

Iraq's attempts to acquire a magnet production plant are likewise ambiguous. Secretary of State Colin Powell stated to the UN Security Council on February 5, 2003 that this plant would produce magnets with a mass of 20 to 30 grams. He added: "That's the same weight as the magnets used in Iraq's gas centrifuge program before the Gulf War." One US official said that because the pieces are so small, many end uses are possible, making it impossible to link the attempted acquisition to an Iraqi centrifuge program.

One piece of intelligence information that seemed to go unnoticed by the media was satellite photographs released by the White House in October [2002] of a facility in Iraq called Al Furat to support Bush's assertion that Iraq was making nuclear weapons there.

But Albright said that Iraq already admitted making such weapons at Al Furat before the Gulf War and that the site had long been dismantled.

In addition to Albright, other military experts also were skeptical of the intelligence information gathered by the CIA.

"Basically, cooked information is working its way into high-level pronouncements and there's a lot of unhappiness about it in intelligence, especially among analysts at the CIA," said Vincent Cannistraro, the CIA's former head of counterintelligence, in an interview with London's *Guardian* newspaper [in] October [2002].

Cannistraro told the *Guardian* that hawks at the Pentagon had deliberately skewed the flow of intelligence to the top levels of the administration.

[In] October [2002], Bush said the Iraqi regime was developing unmanned aerial vehicles [UAV], which "could be used to disperse chemical or biological weapons across broad areas."

"We're concerned that Iraq is exploring ways of using these UAVs for missions targeting the United States," Bush said.

U.S. military experts had confirmed that Iraq had been converting eastern European trainer jets into UAV's, but with a maximum range of a few hundred miles they were no threat to targets in the U.S.

"It doesn't make any sense to me if he meant United States territory," said Stephen Baker, a retired US navy rear admiral who assesses Iraqi military capabilities at the Washington-based Center for Defense Information, also in an interview with the *Guardian* [in] October [2002].

Rushing into War

In true Bush fashion, however, the administration had long believed it was better to strike first and ask questions later.

When Senator Dianne Feinstein, D-California, who sits on the intelligence committee, sent Bush a letter Sept. 17, 2002 requesting he urge the CIA to produce a National Intelligence Estimate, a report that would have showed exactly how much of a threat Iraq posed, Condoleezza Rice, the National Security Adviser, said [that] in the post 9-11 world the U.S. cannot wait for intelligence because the Iraq is too much of a threat to the U.S.

"We don't want the smoking gun to be a mushroom cloud," Rice said.

Can the Proliferation of Weapons of Mass Destruction Be Stopped?

Chapter Preface

When President George W. Bush spoke to a summit of the Group of 8 (the eight industrialized nations considered to be the world's economic leaders) in Poland on May 31, 2003, he introduced a counterproliferation strategy to curb the worldwide dissemination of weapons of mass destruction. The president said of his new plan:

> When weapons of mass destruction or their components are in transit, we must have the means and authority to seize them. So today I announce a new effort to fight proliferation called the Proliferation Security Initiative. The United States and a number of our close allies . . . have begun working on new agreements to search planes and ships carrying suspect cargo and to seize illegal weapons or missile technologies. Over time, we will extend this partnership as broadly as possible to keep the world's most destructive weapons away from our shores and out of the hands of our common enemies.

The Proliferation Security Initiative (PSI) achieved its first major success in 2003 with the interdiction of the *BBC China*, a German-owned ship that was laded with cargo in Dubai, one of the seven states that compose the United Arab Emirates, and headed to Libya. U.S. and British intelligence had been tracking Malaysian-made weapons components delivered to the vessel. When the ship passed through the Suez Canal, German and Italian agencies boarded and uncovered centrifuges that could be used to make nuclear weapons. U.S. and British officials confronted Libya with the evidence, and shortly thereafter, Libyan leader Muammar Ghadafi announced that Libya would no longer seek to produce or deploy WMD.

Critics of the PSI say that it cannot be judged a success unless two of the world's largest states, Russia and China, agree to become members, which they have not done as of

2006. Furthermore, critics have noted that nations intercepting ocean-traveling foreign ships may be violating international law, which could become contentious in the years ahead. Although more than sixty states have agreed in principle to the PSI, a commitment to action is strictly voluntary; the PSI is not a formal treaty. Finally, critics note that the PSI may be another unilateral attempt by the United States to preempt international law by writing its own rules. Such critics tie the PSI to use of preemptive U.S. force, such as the invasion of Iraq in 2003, and the unwillingness of the Bush administration to engage the world through treaty negotiation and diplomacy. The United States, they argue, is once again acting as a superpower, placing its own security interests ahead of the rest of the world's.

Joseph Cirincione and Joshua Williams, writing an assessment for the Carnegie Endowment for International Peace in April 2005, argue that PSI is not a bad idea, it is just a limited one. "Only partnered with more traditional nonproliferation efforts such as the Nuclear Non-Proliferation Treaty can a strengthened and more widely embraced Proliferation Security Initiative help to bring the security that its name invokes," they write.

The PSI is at the heart of the Bush administration's attempt to reengineer counterproliferation in the twenty-first century. The ultimate question is whether WMD proliferation can be stopped by any method. The authors of the following viewpoints offer contradictory opinions in seeking to answer that question.

U.S. Diplomacy Can Halt Nuclear Proliferation and Nuclear Terrorism

Thomas Graham Jr.

Thomas Graham Jr. is the president of the Lawyers Alliance for World Security. He served as ambassador for arms control, nonproliferation, and disarmament under President Bill Clinton.

In addressing the threats of today's world, the United States has before it essentially two lines of approach. One path relies primarily on unilateral diplomatic pressure and, when necessary, preemptive military assault, in some cases without regard to existing treaty obligations or accepted international rules of behavior. Everyone agrees that there are some cases where such a policy is appropriate, such as the military action against Afghanistan following the terrorist attacks of September 11, 2001. But no one would argue that this should always be the path followed in dealing with a serious security threat. For example, with respect to alleged NPT [Nonproliferation Treaty] violations by Iran, the United States has been working through established multilateral institutions such as the IAEA [International Atomic Energy Agency]. There have been few voices urging military confrontation with Iran at this time.

The alternative path thus would be one which emphasizes international cooperation: developing and enforcing international treaty regimes such as the NPT and supporting multilateral institutions. Historically, the United States has been the architect and principal supporter of this approach to international order, and, as the country with the greatest stake in an international order built on treaty relationships, has been the most prominent champion of international law.

Nuclear Nonproliferation Strategies

For over fifty years, the United States pursued a balance of power policy among the great powers—the United States, Russia, China, and Europe. The North Atlantic Treaty Organization and the U.S.-Japan alliance are among the institutions and partnerships created by this grand strategy, the centerpiece of which was containment of the Soviet Union, based on a nuclear deterrence policy which included negotiated arms restraint and which was designed to balance the forces of the two opposing camps. The United States pursued a world order built on rules and international treaties that permitted the expansion of democracy, the enlargement of international security, free market economies, and free trade. Within this international order, in addition to keeping the peace, the United States gave political cover to countries throughout the world to adopt the American position by joining international institutions and multilateral treaty regimes such as the International Telecommunication Union, the World Trade Organization, the Outer Space Treaty, the CFE [Conventional Forces in Europe] Treaty, and the NPT.

The United States has moved ... toward a less cooperative and more unilateral and confrontational strategy.

The Cost of Unilateral Deterrence

However, in recent years the United States has moved away from this world system that it helped to create and toward a less cooperative and more unilateral and confrontational strategy. The United States has rejected new treaty arrangements important to key allies, such as the Kyoto Protocol on global warming and the International Criminal Court, instead of attempting to amend them or leave them quietly "on the shelf." For a long time, we refused direct negotiations with North Korea on their nuclear programs, and we have renounced treaty arrangements that are important to the world community, such as the Anti-Ballistic Missile Treaty and a verification and inspection annex to the Biological Weapons Convention.

John Ikenberry, a distinguished professor of geopolitics at Georgetown University, referred to this new policy approach as "neoimperial." In an article in the September–October 2002 issue of *Foreign Affairs*, he stated that this new policy

> threatens to rend the fabric of the international community and political partnerships precisely at a time when that community and those partnerships are urgently needed. It is an approach fraught with peril and likely to fail. It is not only politically unsustainable, but diplomatically harmful. And if history is a guide, it will trigger antagonism and resistance that will leave America in a more hostile and divided world.

An example would be the National Security Strategy document of September 2002, in which the United States announced a policy of preemptive and preventive war against potential, but not necessarily actual, threats from so-called rogue states and terrorist organizations. Over time, such a policy could strain our economy and our armed forces, and it appears to be wholly destructive of the concept of the rule of law among the states of the world community. A December 2002 addendum on strategy toward threats involving nuclear, chemical, or biological weapons (National Security Strategy to Combat Weapons of Mass Destruction) suggests that force, rather than cooperation and treaty arrangements, is to be the principal means to combat the threat of the proliferation of nuclear weapons and other weapons of mass destruction.

Another example is the most recent Pentagon *Nuclear Posture Review*, submitted in late 2001, which emphasizes the value of nuclear weapons to the United States and implies that we might use them against Iraq, Iran, North Korea, Syria, and Libya (contrary to our NPT pledge, as they were then all NPT nonnuclear weapon states), and also against Russia, as well as China (in defense of Taiwan). Combined with the National Strategy Document, this could create the impression that the United States might someday engage in preemptive or preventive war with the nuclear option on the table.

The answer to the threat of catastrophic terrorism is social, political, economic, and diplomatic.

Countering the Real Danger

As evil, vicious, and corrupt as he was, [Iraqi leader] Saddam Hussein was not the principal threat to the United States—or even a principal threat. Generals Norman Schwarzkopf and Wesley Clark, the military leaders in our previous two major wars, have made clear that the main threats to the United States are Al Qaeda and other international terrorist organizations, combined with nuclear proliferation. These must be our principal focus.

But how best to counteract this danger? Of course, increased vigilance and improved intelligence capabilities are essential. However, using the threat of force as the principal tool to combat proliferation of weapons of mass destruction, as implied by the White House strategy documents, cannot and will not be the long-term answer. Military action can only do so much. The answer to the threat of catastrophic terrorism is social, political, economic, and diplomatic as well as military. In a larger sense, opposition to disease, poverty, and machine gun cultures around the world is as important to national security as military strength. We must be certain that in developing our policies, we are not unduly influenced by purely military considerations. These words from President [Dwight] Eisenhower's farewell address on January 16, 1961, are still relevant:

In the councils of government, we must guard against the acquisition of unwarranted influence, whether sought or unsought, by the military-industrial complex.

The potential for the disastrous rise of misplaced power exists and will persist. We must never let the weight of this combination endanger our liberties or democratic processes. We should take nothing for granted. Only an alert and knowledgeable citizenry can compel the proper meshing of the huge industrial and military machinery of defense with our peaceful methods and goals, so that security and liberty may prosper together.

It is the United States' long-term commitment to multilateral institutions and the rule of law . . . that is important.

A Decisive Bias

In deciding whether to pursue a unilateral or multilateral diplomatic or military solution to a particular international crisis, the problem is not that any particular administration is wholly committed to one course or the other in advance. Obviously, each crisis, each problem has to be analyzed and judged on a case-by-case basis. Rather, the problem is the bias that any administration brings to a question. It is the United States' long-term commitment to multilateral institutions and the rule of law—or the lack thereof—that is important. Will the primary focus of the United States be to build an international system of interlocking treaty regimes and rules to promote international law and defeat aggression and terror, or will the United States place its trust primarily in a doctrine of preemptive war and an enormously capable military establishment? Both views have articulate proponents and most policy makers lean toward one course or the other. But what is to be emphasized? What is to be the bias?

This decision is a fateful one for the world as well as for the United States. The United States has been the most powerful country in the world for a hundred years. For a long time we chose not to use our power. We were late entering World War I, we did not join the League of Nations [precursor to the United Nations], and we were late entering World War II. We opposed colonial empires, and, for the most part, supported international law, open borders, and free trade, but remained isolated behind the two oceans that insulated us. With the close of World War II, however, this policy of isolation changed. The United States founded the United Nations, developed international economic institutions, promoted the NPT and many other international agreements limiting armaments, dismantled our army (the world's strongest in 1945), and did not immediately proceed to build a nuclear arsenal even though we had a monopoly after World War II.

But then came the Cold War, the long, gray struggle between freedom and tyranny that led to the creation of two enormous armed camps and huge stockpiles of nuclear weapons, and which inevitably caused the creation of two large industrial infrastructures to support this heavy investment in a standing military establishment. It also led to the increasing militarization of U.S. society, about which President Eisenhower expressed such grave misgivings.

[Through diplomacy] the twin threats of nuclear proliferation and nuclear terrorism . . . will be lifted.

Defeating Nuclear Proliferation

Throughout the forty-five years of the Cold War, even though there was a military stand-off between the two superpowers, the United States was always the world's preeminent nation, without whose support little was possible. Now, with the collapse of the Soviet Union and the end of the Cold War, the United States is left as the sole surviving superpower—the world's only hyperpower, if you will. The future of the world is largely in our hands. Most diplomats and politicians around the world understand that without the United States in the lead, momentum for international initiatives usually disappears. We must use this power wisely. Unfortunately, other countries are complaining that instead of exhorting the faithful, the preacher himself needs to be reconverted. We are presently engaged in what is likely to be a long, sporadically violent, and dark struggle with the forces of international terrorism and disorder. The United States could choose to go it alone, to rely, when necessary, on the maintenance and quick deployment of our unique military power—the strongest the world has ever seen. But our strength is not limitless, and by failing to act through the world's system of institutions, treaty regimes, and rules, we risk arousing unnecessary opposition and discord in a world community that is almost entirely with us in the war against international terrorism and its associated rogue regimes.

In 1918, what is now Iraq and what is now Iran were made part of the British Empire—the largest empire in history. Even by 1922, it was clear that Britain had overreached. America does not need an empire. It needs peace, cooperation, and the rule of law. This is not a classic war of armies; rather, it is a subtle conflict of culture, economics, diplomacy, intelligence organizations, and sometimes of specially designed military forces. This is a war that can be won as long as the United States—and in the end it always has to be the United States—makes the right choices at the right times. America should return to its historic destiny of keeping the peace and fostering the development of the community of nations, democracies, free market economies, the international rule of law, international institutions, and treaty arrangements. This is both consistent with our principles and our national interest. It is in this way that the twin threats of nuclear proliferation and nuclear terrorism—in the end, the only way that the terrorists can defeat us—will be lifted. And it is in this way that the war on terror can and eventually will be won.

An International Trade Monitoring Agency Could Intercept Weapons of Mass Destruction

Geoffrey Forden

Geoffrey Forden is a research associate with the Science, Technology, and Society Program at the Massachusetts Institute of Technology. He was the analysis section chief for the United Nations WMD Inspection Team in Iraq.

The existence of [former scientific head of Pakistan's nuclear program] Abdul Qadeer Khan's nuclear black market, which supplied entire uranium-enrichment plants to the Libyan nuclear weapons programs, has shocked the world. It should also cause a fundamental rethinking about the frightening speed, nature, and ways further proliferation might occur in the 21st century.

Khan's network, far from being the exception, is likely to prove closer to the rule for how states will try to acquire nuclear, chemical, or biological weapons and related delivery systems in coming years. Rather than slowly developing their own technology or getting assistance from other states, developing countries seeking such weapons can save time, money, and diplomatic capital by buying complete production facilities as well as the know-how to use them from all too many proliferation profiteers.

Yet, although such acquisition pathways afford a state intent on gaining dangerous technology many advantages, they also present the world community with new opportunities for detecting and stopping state proliferation. Such proliferation schemes make use of the same financial instruments as legiti-

Geoffrey Forden, "Avoiding Enrichment: Using Financial Tools to Prevent Another Kahn," *Arms Control Today*, vol. 35, June 2005, pp. 14–15, 17, 19. Reproduced by permission.

mate international trade and leave a tell-tale trail that can be used to detect, stop, or inhibit the efficiency of this proliferation path. Current international nonproliferation regimes could be significantly strengthened if they were buttressed by a dedicated international auditing authority that would track down and investigate suspicious international deals.

A Failing System

Today we rely on customs agents in individual countries to spot the transfer of components for WMD production, an impossible task for individual countries. An international auditing authority, however, could use access to bills of lading, letters of credit, customs reports, and other international trading documentation to unearth the correlation of shipments among purchasers, manufacturers, and trading companies and reconstruct a complete picture of proliferation deals. Private banks wanting to do business with major industrialized countries could be required to grant auditing privileges to the international authority and to do business only with participating banks. Suspicious trade activity could be tagged and examined in detail, including underlying contracts, yielding further insight into suspicious shipments.

Nor do we need to start from scratch in establishing such an authority: the United Nations Monitoring, Verification and Inspection Commission (UNMOVIC) developed experience and expertise in these matters when monitoring Iraq's commercial transactions regarding missile, chemical, and biological technologies. Extending UNMOVIC's mandate to include auditing suspicious letters of credit worldwide could appreciably improve the current nonproliferation regimes.

If international investigators had these tools years ago, they might have fleshed out Khan's activities far before his public confession in February 2004 or the October 2003 intercept of a cargo ship carrying centrifuge components to Libya for use in enriching uranium. That intercept gave U.S. intelligence officials the tangible proof they needed to show that Khan had been secretly selling [the government in Libya's capital] Tripoli centrifuge technology that could help make essential fissile material [weapons-grade uranium and plutonium] for nuclear weapons, although Libya and nearly all of the half-dozen countries involved in the Khan network (with the exception of Pakistan) had acceded to the nuclear Nonproliferation Treaty (NPT).

Developing countries are often familiar with [WMD] deals from acquiring civilian technologies.

Seeking WMD

A state such as Libya, seeking to acquire a militarily significant stockpile of highly dangerous weapons, faces a different task than a terrorist group. In the past, terrorist groups have been satisfied with small quantities of either chemical or biological agents and have not had the capacity to build nuclear weapons. States, on the other hand, are trying to acquire these weapons on an industrial scale and must, therefore, master efficient production techniques. Saddam Hussein's Iraq, for instance, produced 3,000 tons of mustard gas and 8,445 liters of concentrated anthrax.

Hiring a consulting engineering firm to build a complete production facility or licensing the know-how from a proliferation profiteer has clear advantages for a country eager to acquire such weapons. First, it allows a proliferator to acquire production capability quickly and without research and development costs. Second, it is more reliable than other methods such as copying or reverse engineering imported items. Third, international proliferation profiteers can use their business contacts and networks—contacts not associated with a suspect state—to shield their actions from export controls. Finally, developing countries are often familiar with such deals from acquiring civilian technologies.

Libya was apparently aware of these benefits in 1997 when it began its most serious bid to acquire nuclear weapons. That year, Tripoli's representatives met with Khan and his associate, Buhary Syed Abu Tahir, about acquiring a gas centrifuge plant capable of producing weapons-grade enriched uranium. (Tahir also allegedly facilitated Khan's sale of used centrifuge units to Iran in 1994 and 1995 by arranging for their transport.)

It appears that Khan functioned less as a single supplier than [as] the broker for a number of interrelated transactions: Khan supplied designs and specifications, but most of the hardware came from his contacts in other countries. For example, to help put together the gas centrifuges, 300 tons of aluminum tubes and bars were first purchased from a company in Singapore. These semi-finished pieces were then transported to Scomi Precision Engineering (SCOPE) in Malaysia. SCOPE produced several thousand roughly three-feet-long "stationary tubes" and other components. These components were on their way to Libya via a Dubai [capital of the United Arab Emirates] trading company when they were intercepted aboard the freighter *BBC China* in Italy. Other suppliers, operating from Germany, Switzerland, Turkey, and the United Kingdom, also provided electrical components, building designs, and advanced machinery to Libya.

An international auditing agency, with a global view of trades, could more easily spot the significant [WMD] connections.

It is clear that Libya was acquiring an entire enrichment facility and a machine shop capable of repairing broken units. Reports by the International Atomic Energy Agency state that Libya placed an order for 10,000 additional second-generation units, sufficient to enrich enough uranium for nearly 15 bombs per year. They also indicate that Khan's associates were not only involved in the training of Libyan workers in the use of the advanced machinery but were likely to have given instructions in the workings of a centrifuge plant.

Locating Black Market WMD

Why were so many components allowed to be made and shipped? Why were customs officials not able to stop vital centrifuge components from leaving their countries? According to Malaysia's inspector general, the Khan network was able to disguise shipment destinations and split the manufacture of critical components among different companies and even different countries. This obscured the magnitude of the operation. To quote the Malaysian report, "[W]ithout knowing the full or a significant portion of the total subassembly, no definitive [assessment] of the possible device may be made." . . .

In today's world, such a scheme, with so many different companies and front companies, can be hidden from national customs agents. This is likely to still prove the case even if all states fully implement UN Security Council Resolution 1540. The measure, approved [in 2004], calls on all states to take steps to improve their export control regimes in order to prevent terrorists from gaining access to nuclear, chemical, or biological weapons and related materials. An international auditing agency, with a global view of trades, could more easily spot the significant connections between high-strength tubes and components purchased from other companies in other countries. It could do this by comparing both shipments' bills of lading, letters of credit, and customs reports because they can track them to their ultimate destination and trace them back to their original purchasers.

In the case of Khan's transshipment of SCOPE centrifuge tubes in Dubai, such an agency might have quickly detected the ultimate destination by noting that no customs reports were filed when they arrived at their first port. This is just one example of using a port's material balance—adding up all the items coming into and leaving the port—to spot the diversion of goods. The international auditing agency could use such procedures to detect other tricks the proliferator might try, such as altering the tubes' bill of lading during transshipment in Dubai to disguise their high-strength aluminum properties.

If these actions can be carried out in real time, the auditing agency can alert the relevant customs agencies and, if those agencies request expert assistance, could inspect the suspect shipments. If it proves impossible to correlate all the relevant pieces of documentation fast enough for such an intervention, the auditing agency can still perform a valuable service. It can alert the world to a potential proliferation problem allowing concerned states to initiate sanctions or other nonproliferation actions. The case for such sanctions will be much stronger and the debate more focused on policy rather than disputed facts because of the international auditing agency's efforts.

Intelligence services from supporting governments can also call the auditing authority's attention to specific trades.

Analyzing WMD Records

To be sure, there are practical and political problems associated with the auditing authority proposed here. On the political side, some might find a comprehensive international regime objectionable no matter what safeguards are taken to preserve confidentiality. Of course, this point of view ignores the fact that numerous individuals in international banking and insurance institutions already see this information. Nonetheless, some are sure to object to creating any international agency with broad oversight authority. If that view prevails, there will be nothing but voluntary associations of "supplier" countries to stem the tide of proliferation. Although these supplier regimes play an important role, they do not have a global view to detect components for complete facilities manufactured in different parts of the world.

If a truly functioning authority is to be created, some practical issues will also need to be addressed. In particular, auditing the world's trade of manufactured goods could imply reviewing 20 million trades per year, an apparently monumental task. Yet, modern information technology makes this feasible. Once the documents have been entered into the computer, an automatic pattern recognition program can flag questionable deals for attention by human analysts. Furthermore, the intelligence services from supporting governments can also call the auditing authority's attention to specific trades, greatly simplifying the recognition problem. It should be remembered that UNMOVIC reviewed Iraq's imports during the period of the Goods Review List.

In fact, the largest problem is not analyzing all these records but obtaining them in electronic format. Currently, only a small but growing percentage of these trades use electronically formatted bills of lading and letters of credit. Therefore, the principal bottleneck will be scanning in the documents and converting them to computer-readable forms.

A new proliferation auditing authority stands a good chance of . . . detecting and preventing proliferation.

A final objection might be raised by analysts concerned that proliferators will simply bypass the international trade instruments that have been carefully worked out over the years to protect both trading partners. It is true that proliferators could bypass this nonproliferation regime in such a fashion. In fact, government-to-government proliferators can clearly avoid this regime altogether. Such proliferation is presumably handled exclusively through national banks that do not have the same financial incentives that private banks have to submit copies of letters of credit and other documentation to the auditing authority. Many of the recent examples of proliferation, however, have occurred with governments purchasing packaged technologies from private entities, which do not have their own banks and would hesitate to deal in cash. After all, both parties give up a considerable amount of security when they bypass international institutions, which makes procurement efforts that much more difficult. Many companies that would otherwise be willing to contribute to the production of weapons of mass destruction might not if they lacked the standard guarantees.

Detection and Prevention

Iraq, even during the height of sanctions, did not completely give up standard trade mechanisms. Instead, the Iraq Survey Group has found that Iraq would either pay cash to intermediaries who signed letters of credit or used nominee-named letters of credit to obscure that the goods were destined for Iraq. Thus, a new proliferation auditing authority stands a good chance of either detecting and preventing proliferation or inhibiting proliferation by forcing proliferators to work outside all the established mechanisms for international trade.

The United States Is Winning the War Against Weapons of Mass Destruction Proliferation

John R. Bolton

John R. Bolton is the U.S. ambassador to the United Nations. Previously, he served the George W. Bush administration as undersecretary for arms control and international security.

Some supporters of "multilateralism" [diplomacy among many nations] prefer to talk about its glories in the abstract rather than take action in the here and now. The [George W.] Bush administration's nonproliferation policies fall into the latter category. Rather than rely on cumbersome treaty-based bureaucracies, this administration has launched initiatives that involve cooperative action with other sovereign states to deny rogue nations and terrorists access to the materials and know-how needed to develop weapons of mass destruction (WMD). Our policies show that robust use of the sovereign authorities we and our allies possess can produce real results.

Reinventing Nonproliferation

The Bush administration is reinventing the nonproliferation regime it inherited, crafting policies to fill gaping holes, reinforcing earlier patchwork fixes, assembling allies, creating precedents and changing perceived realities and stilted legal thinking. The frontlines in our nonproliferation strategy must extend beyond the well-known rogue states to the trade routes and entities engaged in supplying proliferant countries. This can properly be described not as "nonproliferation," but as "counterproliferation." To accomplish this, we are making more robust use of existing authorities, including sanctions, interdiction and credible export controls. Most importantly, we have taken significant steps to improve coordination between sovereign states to act against proliferators.

Sovereign states are responsible for ... closing the loopholes exploited by black market WMD networks.

As we learned from the unravelling of the clandestine nuclear weapons network run by [former Pakistani nuclear weapons chief] A.Q. Khan and from the Libyan WMD programme, proliferators employ increasingly sophisticated and aggressive measures to obtain WMD or missile-related materials. They rely heavily on front companies and illicit brokers in their quest for arms, equipment, sensitive technology and dual-use goods.

Closing Proliferation Loopholes

In his September 2003 speech to the United Nations General Assembly, George W. Bush proposed that the Security Council pass a resolution calling on member states to criminalise WMD proliferation, enact export controls and secure sensitive materials within their borders. The resulting Security Council Resolution 1540, unanimously adopted, achieved the president's goals. Rather than requiring years negotiating treaties and creating elaborate institutions, Resolution 1540 rests on the notion that sovereign states are responsible for writing and implementing laws closing the loopholes exploited by black market WMD networks.

Among the most prominent of this administration's counterproliferation innovations is the Proliferation Security Initiative (PSI). We say that PSI is "an activity, not an organization," in this case an activity designed to halt trafficking in WMD, their delivery systems and related materials. In developing PSI, our main goal has been a simple one: to enable practical cooperation among states to help navigate this increasingly challenging arena. The initiative focuses on enhancing states' operational capabilities in the intelligence, military and law enforcement arenas. More than 60 countries gathered in Poland [in 2004] to mark PSI's one-year anniversary—and some notable successes. The interception, in cooperation with the U.K., Germany, and Italy, of the *BBC China*, a vessel loaded with nuclear-related components, helped convince Libya that the days of undisturbed accumulation of WMD were over, and helped unravel A.Q. Khan's network.

[The United States is] no longer lost in endless international negotiations whose point seems to be negotiation rather than decision.

Another important administration initiative is the Global Partnership Against the Spread of Weapons and Materials of Mass Destruction, launched by the Group of Eight [aka G-8, a collective of eight industrial nations bound by trading and security policies] at its June 2002 summit. Here again, this effort relies on the commitments of sovereign states acting separately and in concert to secure sensitive materials. Like PSI, the Global Partnership is an activity, not an organization. The G-8 Leaders and 13 additional partners have pledged to raise up to $20bn [billion] (£11.3bn) over 10 years for projects to prevent dangerous weapons and materials from falling into the wrong hands.

Winning the War on Proliferation

The U.S. already has nonproliferation projects under way not only in Russia but in Ukraine, Kazakhstan, Uzbekistan, Georgia, and other former Soviet states, as do other Global Partnership countries. We recently began assistance in Iraq and Libya and are encouraging our partners to undertake their own projects in such states. At [the] Sea Island [Georgia, nuclear summit in 2004], the G-8 agreed to use the Global Partnership to coordinate activities in these areas.

This administration is working to make up for decades of stillborn plans, wishful thinking and irresponsible passivity. We're already late, but we are no longer bystanders wringing our hands and hoping that somehow we will find shelter from gathering threats. We are no longer lost in endless international negotiations whose point seems to be negotiation rather than decision, and no longer waiting beneath the empty protection of a reluctant international body while seeking grudging permission to take measures to protect ourselves.

Not only are we meeting this ultimate of threats on the field, we are advancing on it . . . successfully.

Mr. Bush has begun laying the foundation for a comprehensive, root-and-branch approach to the mortal danger of the proliferation of instruments intended for our destruction. We are determined to use every resource at our disposal— using diplomacy regularly, economic pressure when it makes a difference, active law enforcement when appropriate and military force when we must.

We are just at the beginning, but it is an extraordinary beginning. Not only are we meeting this ultimate of threats on the field, we are advancing on it, battling not only aggressively, but successfully. And so we must, for the outcome of this battle may hold nothing less than the chance to survive.

The Proliferation of Weapons of Mass Destruction Cannot Be Reversed

Steven LaTulippe

Steven LaTulippe is an Ohio physician and a regular contributor to LewRockwell.com, a libertarian opinion Web site.

In the first presidential debate [of the 2004 election campaign] . . . both [George W. Bush and John Kerry were asked] for their opinions as to what single issue represented the gravest threat to America's national security. Both candidates responded that the proliferation of weapons of mass destruction [WMDs] was clearly the most serious. . . .

It may seem a bit odd, and perhaps ironic, that the greatest danger to America derives from the attitudes of our own rulers, but I am nevertheless convinced that this is so. Since the end of the cold war, America's elites have become imbued with the idea that we are "the last remaining superpower" and that we should strive for "benevolent world hegemony." This policy has numerous inevitable negative repercussions with which we are now coping on a daily basis.

There is further irony to be found when one realizes that this attitude is totally at odds with our nation's past history and character. Clearly, even a cursory reading of the opinions of our Founders indicates that they believed that America should be an example to all, but should otherwise eschew "going forth in search of monsters to destroy."

Having discarded the sage advice of our Founders, the current political elites have placed our nation in a serious jeopardy that is significantly worse than would otherwise be the case—far more so than would result from the proliferation of WMDs alone.

Steven LaTulippe, "America's National Security: The Greatest Danger," LewRockwell. com, October 11, 2004. Reproduced by permission.

Proliferation Is Inevitable

I base this opinion on several conclusions:

The doctrine of pre-emption is pointless, since we cannot prevent WMD proliferation.

WMDs will continue to become more widespread. . . . This process cannot be reversed.

Part of the messiah complex that haunts our rulers' psyche is the idea that our government is omnipotent. Listening to the debates, it quickly became clear to me that our leaders believe that literally everything is achievable by our government. The feds now hold that every imaginable issue, both domestic and foreign, can be addressed and perfected by the actions of Washington. They acknowledge literally no limitations on that power. Even the suggestion of practical limits draws angry retorts of "defeatism" and "lack of imagination and willpower." Despite repeated failures, from the war on drugs to the ongoing basket-case of our federalized public schools, our politicos persist in this grand delusion.

But the realities of WMDs are much more complex. Whether any of us like it or not, WMDs will continue to become more widespread. The technology for developing nuclear, chemical, and biological weapons is spreading to all corners of the globe. This process cannot be reversed. Any well-trained microbiologist can manufacture bioweapons in a small, discrete lab which can be hidden almost anywhere. Chemical weapons manufacturing is almost as easy and nearly as undetectable.

If we embrace an ideology that any nation developing such weapons should be threatened or invaded, we will quickly find ourselves in a futile, quixotic crusade that is destined to fail. Even *ideal* intelligence will frequently be incorrect. September 11 [2001] and the intelligence debacle concerning Iraqi WMDs demonstrates that intelligence is usually far from ideal.

Attempts to appoint ourselves the global WMD police will result in our becoming the planetary bully and busybody, since such a role can only be accomplished by policies deemed humiliating and intrusive by the rest of the globe.

This will not be successful in containing the spread of these weapons, but it will be successful in breeding enormous hatred and contempt for America and consequently seriously imperil the safety of our citizenry.

Dictators and WMDs: Just because they have them doesn't mean they'll use them.

One of the major arguments for our new role as globocop is the argument that dictators who gain access to WMDs will likely use them against us. Thus, we have no choice but to act aggressively against any despot who we believe is developing them.

This is simply not true.

[Nazi Germany's leader] Adolf Hitler, for instance, possessed a large stockpile of chemical weapons throughout [World War] II. But even up to the bitter end, he did not deploy them. [Communist Soviet leader] Joseph Stalin had huge stockpiles of nuclear, chemical, and biological weapons. Yet he never used them against the United States either.

And Hitler and Stalin were pretty bad actors, even as dictators go.

Aggressive warmongering often incites that which it is designed to prevent.

Aggression Produces More WMD

The most obvious reason that they did not use WMDs was that they feared retaliation. While dictators are evil, they are usually not flagrantly suicidal. Saddam [Hussein's] use of WMDs against the United States, for instance, would have been the signing of his own (and Iraq's) death warrant. He knew this, and consequently never utilized them.

Thus, we need not prosecute an endless series of preemptive wars against any nation suspected of building WMDs just to avoid having them used against us.

Deterrence works, and it's a lot more reasonable of a foreign policy than condemning our nation to the endless warfare which the doctrine of pre-emption necessitates.

While one can argue that any given dictator *might* use WMDs against America, one can also create scenarios for virtually any danger. Who is to say that rogue Russian soldiers *might* not launch a missile against us? Perhaps the Chinese will accidentally launch one? Perhaps Pakistan's government will be overthrown and replaced by Islamic militants, who will subsequently gain control of their nuclear arsenal? There can be no end to speculation as to what *might* happen anywhere at anytime. And a foreign policy founded on such speculation literally implies war without end.

Aggressive warmongering often incites that which it is designed to prevent.

The Middle East is currently experiencing a high fever of militant Islamism. This is occurring for a wide variety of reasons and has been the subject of much debate. But whatever the cause, one thing is clear: Fundamentalist Islam is not a credible, long-term ideology around which a modern nation can be constructed. A productive economy with prosperous citizens cannot be sustained by the tenets of radical Islam. It is destined to fail, just like communism was destined to fail.

This fever will pass.

The only real issue is how we will interact with the Middle East as it goes through this period of crisis, and what the resulting repercussions will be.

Aggressive American militarism aimed at Muslim countries will be profoundly counterproductive for both the indigenous forces of modernity found there and for America's own safety and security.

Take the example of Iran. That nation was the first to enter the long, dark tunnel of Muslim Fundamentalism. The rise of the mullah-dominated government occurred back in the 1970s, after the fall of the Shah. By the 1990s, the clear majority of the population had become totally disillusioned with this form of government and was clamoring for change. Riots were breaking out and the fundamentalists appeared to be losing their grip on power.

We were on the cusp of a profound moment in history. The first nation to have an Islamist government (in modern times) was becoming increasingly destabilized by its own population's demand for reform and modernity.

Our bellicose jihad against WMDs has profoundly worsened the situation [in Iran].

Then along came the neocons [neoconservatives].

Once President [George W.] Bush started his "axis of evil" malarkey, the surging demands for reform in Iran immediately subsided. After Bush invaded Iraq and continued to threaten Iran, the people of Iran rallied nationalistically behind their government. They closed ranks against an external threat, as people always do. Those reformers who are still active in Iran are widely discredited for their associations with America.

A crucial moment in history was lost. The American people would have been much better off had our government stayed out of Iran altogether and allowed events to take their natural course. The people of the Middle East may well then have occupied a front-row seat from which to watch a fundamentalist nation making the transition to true democracy.

Instead, the mullahs [Islamic clergy] are now more entrenched than ever.

Our bellicose jihad [holy war] against WMDs has profoundly worsened the situation there because the reinvigorated and hostile Iranian government is now nearing the final stages of building nuclear weapons.

Our militarism has achieved the exact opposite of its stated intent.

What gives America the right to arbitrarily decide that other sovereign nations may not possess [WMDs]?

A Pre-emptive Pandora's Box

The doctrine of unilateral pre-emption cannot credibly be claimed solely by America.

In the run-up to the Iraq invasion, the much-reviled [French president] Jacques Chirac vehemently stated that the doctrine of unilateral pre-emption would introduce a catastrophic instability into the world system.

Even a casual analysis demonstrates this to be true. President Bush is essentially claiming that America may invade any nation at any time on the mere suspicion of developing WMDs.

This brings up two obvious problems.

First, what gives America the right to arbitrarily decide that other sovereign nations may not possess these weapons? It may be self-evident to the Washington elite that Algeria or Brazil should not build nuclear weapons, but are they [Algeria and Brazil] not justified in asking just who made America the Big Boss? We have nukes, as do many other nations—so why can't they?

Second, why can't other nations who feel threatened by a neighboring country invoke the same unilateral pre-emption that Bush claims? India has a real concern about Pakistan's nuclear program. The Middle East is rife with mistrust and feuds between various governments, as is Africa and parts of Asia. [In September 2004], South Korea admitted to having performed experiments to develop weapons-grade nuclear material. Should North Korea now invade the South based on pre-emptive defense?

Since Bush did what he did [invade Iraq], he has set a terrible example for the rest of the planet. And he has opened a Pandora's Box which will spew forth many horrible things in the future.

A WMD Moral Calculus

America is acting in ways which are guaranteed to produce mass casualties now for the purpose of preventing hypothetical ones in the future.

Using the doctrine of pre-emption, the Bush Administration has embarked on the invasion of Iraq and has threatened similar action against a host of other nations from Iran to North Korea. The essence of the argument behind this doctrine is that America can no longer wait for rogue nations to develop WMDs, since they may use these weapons against us directly or give them to terrorist groups. This argument was best enunciated by [former] NSC [National Security Council] advisor Condoleezza Rice when she famously stated that we "don't want the smoking gun to be a mushroom cloud."

The problem with this argument is that it virtually guarantees that America will become involved in a variety of preventative wars. These wars will have immediate, predictable casualty rates for both American soldiers and the citizens of those lands which we invade. The Iraq War, for instance, has already resulted in over 1000 American battle deaths, several times that many injuries, and tens of thousands of Iraqi deaths.

This creates a morally inexcusable "casualty algebra" that is the inevitable consequence of this doctrine. We are embarking on these wars because of the *hypothetical possibility* that America may suffer thousands of casualties from a WMD attack sometime in the *indefinite future*. But in so doing, we are causing thousands of *actual* casualties *now*. And given the difficulty in deploying many WMDs (particularly biological and chemical weapons), our invasion of Iraq may well have already killed more civilians than would be lost in a hypothetical terror attack.

The tens of thousands of Iraqi civilians who have died thus far in this war were innocent human beings. Their death is very real, while the probability that Saddam would have used WMDs against us (even if he did, in fact, have them) must be considered very remote.

This policy is thus deeply intellectually flawed and morally indefensible.

Our foreign policy has drastically increased the possibility that we will suffer a mass terror attack.

Hurting America

The ideology of interventionism in general, and the doctrine of pre-emption in particular, are America's single greatest national security threat.

The Founding Fathers were vehement in their belief that American should "extend the hand of friendship and commerce to all, but entangling alliances with none." They believed that the purpose of our government was to "ensure the blessings of liberty for ourselves and our posterity." *A nation dedicated to this policy would not likely be the target of a terror attack since groups involved in various disputes would have no real reason to do so.*

The current elite culture in America has totally abandoned this doctrine. We now station American troops in over 100 nations scattered all across the globe. We have inserted ourselves into parochial [local] conflicts in every inhabited continent on the planet. We have claimed the unilateral right to strike anywhere at anytime, even when we are not being explicitly threatened.

Consequently, America is now seen as a belligerent in all of these wars. Thus, we have given the antagonists in these conflicts the motive to launch attacks against us. And since we cannot ultimately prevent the proliferation of WMDs, our foreign policy has drastically increased the possibility that we will suffer a mass terror attack.

Even more tragic is the fact that our government, having engaged in these policies, is now trying to prevent just such an attack by militarizing our society and stripping Americans of their Constitutional rights. In what can only be described as a horrible "feedback loop," our government is depriving us of our precious liberties in order to prevent attacks which that very same government's policies have gone so far to provoke.

And as icing on the cake, the doctrine of interventionism is helping to hurtle our nation towards bankruptcy. The cost of a global military, various pre-emptive wars, and homeland security have helped to explode our annual deficit to nearly half a trillion dollars per year.

Our nation's reputation, finances, and liberty are thus all being compromised by this pernicious ideology. And taken together, it easily represents the gravest threat to our Republic and our way of life—far greater than the development of WMDs by various remote nations ever could.

Nuclear Proliferation Will Continue As Nations Try to Acquire Deterrence Capabilities

Mirza Aslam Beg

Mirz Aslam Beg is a general in and the former chief of staff of the Pakistani army.

Early [in 2004] when Abdul Qadeer Khan [former head of Pakistan's nuclear program and a nuclear black marketeer] was targeted for alleged nuclear proliferation, I was also implicated and remained under the world media's focus.

During an NBC TV network interview, I was asked the question whether I would like my future generations to live in this part of the world, which is threatened by nuclear holocaust.

I said: Yes, certainly, I would like my future generations to live in South Asia where I see no threat of nuclear war, because perfect nuclear deterrence holds between India and Pakistan. But certainly I would not like my future generations to live in the neighborhood of "nuclear capable Israel."

He questioned: In that case would you like to pass on the nuclear capability to Iran, which considers itself threatened by Israel? I said no. Countries acquire the capability on their own, as we have done it.

Iran will do the same, because they are threatened by Israel. The media hype and the consequences of the reported nuclear proliferation, led to the tormenting treatment meted out to Khan.

Proliferation Is Exported by the United States

For a long time, Americans and Europeans have been engaged in nuclear proliferation, as part of a concept, called "outsourcing nuclear capability," to friendly countries as a measure of defense against nuclear strikes. The concept is interesting as well as regrettable.

The Natural Resource Defense Council of the United States reveals in its report that: "A specific number of nuclear warheads, under U.S. and NATO [North Atlantic Treaty Organization] war plans, will be transferred to America's non-nuclear allies to be delivered to targets by their warplanes.

'Enlightened nuclear proliferation' [is] being implemented by those who are responsible for [the] nuclear non-proliferation regime.

"Preparations for delivering 180 nuclear bombs are taking place in peacetime, and equipping non-nuclear countries with the means to conduct nuclear warfare, (which) is inconsistent with today's international efforts to dissuade other countries from obtaining nuclear weapons.

"The arsenal is being kept at eight Air Force bases in Belgium, Germany, Italy, the Netherlands, Turkey and Britain. The strike plans' potential targets are Russia and countries in the Middle East—most likely Iran and Syria."

Innocent Nuclear Proliferation

It would be appropriate to call this concept an "enlightened nuclear proliferation" being implemented by those who are responsible for [the] nuclear non-proliferation regime.

After the breakup of the Soviet Union [in 1991], nuclear scientists and nuclear material of all kinds proliferated: "Half of the nuclear materials, pieces and parts of it, are unaccounted for by the Russians—and a lot of them are at places in rural areas, which is more threatening to the world right now."

India, "according to international media—February 2004, reported 25 cases of 'missing' or 'stolen' radioactive material from its labs to the International Atomic Energy Agency. Fifty-two percent of the cases were attributed to 'theft' and 48 percent to 'missing mystery.' India claimed to have recovered lost material in 12 of the total 25 cases." How innocently simple is the way of "innocent nuclear proliferation."

The Nuclear Fault Line of the Twenty-First Century

For quite a while, North Korea has been complaining about nuclear warheads placed in South Korea by the United States, which prompted North Korea to develop its own nuclear weapons capability.

In Pakistan's neighborhood, Iran is under tremendous pressure for allegedly attempting to develop the nuclear weapons, which Iran has denied. The war of nerves between the United States and Iran thus has been going on for quite sometime.

On Feb. 16 [2005] very disturbing news was splashed on a Pakistani private TV channel, picked up from Tehran [Iran] Radio, that 12 of the suspected Iranian nuclear sites had been hit by missiles.

The news was really alarming but gradually it transpired that some rock blasting occurred in the southern region of Iran, which was taken as missile attacks.

Whether the news was fake or prompted, it did help Iran test the nerves of the United States and Israel, because both promptly denied that any such strike was carried out. Thus deterrence between Iran and Israel now ... appears to have crossed the threshold of ambiguity, which, indeed is significant.

While Iran has tested the nerves of its adversaries, North Korea has corrected the imbalance in South East Asia by declaring its capability. Since both are termed "rogue states," it would be proper to call it "rogue nuclear proliferation."

The nuclear non-proliferation regime ... is dying its natural death.

Nuclear deterrence between Iran and Israel has crossed the psychological barrier. Nuclear deterrence between South and North Korea has already been established.

Therefore, the nuclear fault line of the 21st century now extends from Israel to Iran, Pakistan to India and South Korea to North Korea, while the strategic balance is held by the United States and Europe on one side and Russia and China on the other.

The New Nuclear Security Paradigm

The nuclear non-proliferation regime, therefore, is dying its natural death at the hands of those who are the exponents of the nuclear non-proliferation regime.

'Enlightened proliferators,' together with ... 'rogue proliferators,' would democratize the global nuclear non-proliferation order.

How the new balance of terror will be maintained from Mediterranean to Pacific is a task for those who, having themselves violated the nuclear proliferation regime, are now responsible for maintaining global nuclear peace.

The world now has to wait and see how objectives of the utopian nuclear non-proliferation regime are achieved.

At the beginning of the new era, the emerging multipolar world order is facing the formidable challenge of a dangerous global nuclear security paradigm.

Fortunately, the emerging multipolar global order is expected to be less confrontational than the bipolar world order [between the USSR and the United States during the Cold War] and less brutal and tyrannical than the unipolar world order of today [in which the United States dominates].

With at least six competing geo-economic centers of power, the new world order would be more democratic in nature as it would be governed by forces of globalization and integrative economic demands.

Such democratization of the world order will bring sanity into the entire gambit of nuclear proliferation. The "enlightened proliferators," together with the "innocent" and the "rogue proliferators," would democratize the global nuclear non-proliferation order. This may be the only hope for all living beings inhabiting this wretched earth.

The United States Believes Bioweapons Proliferation Is Unstoppable

Mark Wheelis and Malcolm Dando

Mark Wheelis teaches microbiology at the University of California–Davis. Malcolm Dando is professor of international security at the University of Bradford, England, and the author of New Biological Weapons: Threat, Proliferation, and Control.

In the summer of 2001, the United States shocked its peers when it rejected the protocol to the bioweapons treaty. Intended to strengthen compliance with the vital but weak Biological Weapons Convention (BWC), the protocol was dead in the water without U.S. support, and the world was left wondering what prompted the surprise move.

Some suggest the rejection was due to changing U.S. perceptions of sovereignty and self-reliance. Others thought that perhaps its own . . . covert biological programs were too sensitive for the United States to willingly reveal more. But this explanation falls short because, had it wished, the United States could have both supported the protocol and avoided disclosing its secret operations simply by terminating them before the protocol entered into force.

A more ominous explanation is that perhaps the United States rejected the protocol not just because it is conducting secret, offensively oriented "biodefense" programs, but because it is committed to continuing and expanding them.

The Treaty and Its Protocol

The BWC, signed in 1972 and entered into force in 1975, was the first treaty to ban the possession of an entire class of

Mark Wheelis and Malcolm Dando, "Back to Bioweapons?" *Bulletin of the Atomic Scientists*, vol. 59, January/February 2003, pp. 40–46. Copyright © 2003 by The Educational Foundation for Nuclear Science, Chicago, IL 60637. Reproduced by permission of Bulletin of the Atomic Scientists: The Magazine of Global Security News & Analysis.

weapons of mass destruction. It prohibits the development, production, and stockpiling of microorganisms or toxins for other than peaceful purposes, and it categorically prohibits development, production, and stockpiling of devices designed to disseminate such agents for hostile purposes. It is a landmark in weapons control.

The bioweapons treaty . . . has essentially no verification provisions, and there have been notable violations.

But the bioweapons treaty lacks teeth. It has essentially no verification provisions, and there have been notable violations. The Soviet Union (and later Russia) maintained a massive stockpile of biological agents and delivery devices into the 1990s. Iraq's modest stockpile of agents and munitions was discovered by a U.N. inspection team in 1995. And classified intelligence suggests that several other nations either have or are pursuing offensive biowarfare capabilities. Among them are Israel, North Korea, Iran, Syria, Libya, and China.

The treaty's failure to prevent proliferation led to the start of negotiations in 1995 for an addendum to the treaty—a protocol that would establish legally binding measures to promote compliance. Major elements included:

- Annual declarations that would require participating nations to identify and describe their biodefense facilities and programs, as well as industrial facilities that could be used to produce microbial cultures in quantity.

- Random visits to declared facilities. A consultation process would be provided if one country questioned the completeness or accuracy of another's declarations.

- A provision for a multilateral team to conduct short-notice investigations into facilities suspected of illegally producing bioweapons agents, allegations of bioweapons use, or disease outbreaks suspected to be the result of an accidental release of microbes from an illegal facility.

By mid-2001 a consensus text was emerging, and on July 23, 2001, the twenty-fourth negotiating session convened. Delegates expected their efforts would soon result in a final text. During the first three days, more than 50 nations spoke in favor of promptly completing the negotiations. Then U.S. [ambassador] Donald Mahley brought the entire process to an end: "The United States has concluded that the current approach to a protocol to the Biological Weapons Convention . . . is not, in our view, capable of . . . strengthening confidence in compliance with the Biological Weapons Convention. . . . We will therefore be unable to support the current text, even with changes."

Without U.S. participation, few other countries could be expected to sign on. Its surprise announcement cost the United States a great deal of goodwill. This ill-will was compounded later in 2001 when, at the Fifth Review Conference, the United States tried at the last minute to terminate protocol negotiations completely, throwing the meeting into disorder and leaving no option but to suspend the conference. . . .

U.S. Reasons for Non-compliance

Why did the United States take such dramatic and unpopular action so late in the game? Why did the United States, unlike any of its principal allies, supposedly decide that the protocol would not enhance its security? What about the protocol was so threatening that it justified tearing a serious rift between the United States and its closest allies?

The United States gave three reasons. First, it said, the protocol couldn't adequately detect secret bioweapons proliferation. It is true that a single inspection may not be enough to discriminate between a covert program and a legitimate biotech operation. But this limitation was understood from the start. The true value of the protocol was expected to be the increased transparency it would bring to worldwide biodefense and biotech activities. Frequent routine visits, coupled with the possibility of an intrusive investigation to resolve specific suspicions, were thought to be a significant deterrent to all but the most determined proliferator. No verification measure could ever absolutely guarantee the detection of all covert biowarfare activity, but the protocol was seen by all close U.S. allies as a modest improvement in short-term security whose value would increase substantially with time.

Another reason the United States gave for rejecting the protocol was that it would unacceptably jeopardize commercial proprietary secrets. Yet the protocol had been drafted to specifically protect such industrial information: All visits and investigations would be conducted under rules of managed access, meaning that the visited facility could shroud equipment, block access to certain areas, turn off computer monitors, and take other measures necessary to protect its proprietary secrets. Unlike its allies, the United States made little effort to work with its industries to test whether the visits and inspections envisaged under the protocol would work. Several other countries, individually and in collaboration, made numerous trial visits to different industrial sites. The results were clear—visits could effectively verify declarations and increase confidence in treaty compliance without putting industrial secrets at risk. . . .

The third reason the United States gave for rejecting the protocol was that it would endanger its biodefense program. This too is puzzling. Most of the principal allies of the United States have biodefense programs—some of them quite substantial—and they all concluded that their programs would not be compromised. Furthermore, the U.S. biodefense program has traditionally been largely unclassified. It is hard to see how such a program could be seriously compromised by visits and investigations—unless the historical openness of the program has recently changed.

None of the explanations the United States gave sufficiently justifies such a diplomatically costly step, nor are they consistent with the broad support the protocol had from countries with proliferation concerns, biotech and pharmaceutical industries, and biodefense programs similar to the United States. The only area in which it is plausible that the United States differs significantly from its allies is its recent classified biodefense activities.

Investigation into the [2001] anthrax letter attacks revealed that the United States had an ongoing program to produce dried, weaponized anthrax spores.

An Ongoing U.S. Bioweapons Program

After [President Richard] Nixon renounced offensive bioweapons programs, the biodefense program was essentially unclassified. Housed mainly in the U.S. Army Medical Research Institute for Infectious Diseases, its only classified portion was a small, analytical (not experimental) threat analysis component. Now the Energy Department, Defense Department, and even the CIA conduct classified biodefense programs. When this change began—and why—is unclear. It appears to have begun early in the [Bill] Clinton administration, at a time when government concerns about bioweapons in the hands of terrorists were growing and agencies' roles in the post–Cold War world were changing. Presumably most of the new programs are legitimate defensive work, but in fall 2001 several programs that may have violated the bioweapons treaty were revealed—and it is likely that others remain closeted.

One of the uncovered projects, run by the CIA, involved building and testing a cluster munition, modeled on a Soviet bioweapon, to spread biological agents. Another secret project, under the Pentagon's Defense Threat Reduction Agency, tested whether terrorists could construct a sophisticated bioweapon plant from commercially available materials without raising suspicions. Project personnel bought the supplies, built the facility, and used it to produce nonpathogenic bacterial spores that were then dried and weaponized. A third project was to be administered by the Defense Intelligence Agency, another Pentagon unit, but it may not have gone beyond the planning stage. It was to have genetically engineered *Bacillus anthracis* (the causative agent of anthrax) to re-create a Soviet strain thought to be resistant to the U.S. vaccine.

It seems the U.S. government has concluded that the global proliferation of bioweapons is inevitable.

In addition, the investigation into the [2001] anthrax letter attacks [against two U.S. senators and several media outlets] revealed that the United States had an ongoing program to produce dried, weaponized anthrax spores for defensive testing. How much was made is unclear, but multiple production runs were apparently conducted over many years, and total production must have been in the 10s or 100s of grams of dried anthrax spores. Since a single gram of anthrax spores contains millions of lethal doses, the quantities produced seem unjustifiable for peaceful purposes under the bioweapons treaty. Whether excess spores were stockpiled or destroyed—or whether they can even be adequately accounted for—is unknown.

Under the treaty's confidence-building measures, agreed to in 1986, the United States made a commitment to annually declare all its biodefense projects and facilities. None of the above programs was mentioned in U.S. declarations.

An Unstoppable U.S. Bioweapons Proliferation

It seems the U.S. government has concluded that the global proliferation of bioweapons is inevitable. Having made this decision, the United States may have concluded that an offensive biological research program was necessary to evaluate the threat, devise countermeasures, and possibly even to eventually develop sophisticated bioweapons. Perhaps this decision follows from secret policy responding to known instances of bioweapons proliferation, or perhaps from a convergent belief in the biothreat among those with policy responsibility in different agencies. [The terrorist attacks of] September 11 and the anthrax letter attacks lent urgency and credibility to this position, and also sparked greatly expanded funding for biodefense work.

The U.S belief that bioweapons proliferation is unstoppable, paired with its long-standing belief that its security is based on technological superiority, may very well lead to the exploration of biotech applied to bioweapons development, with serious implications for arms control. The consequences threaten to fatally undermine both the bioweapons and chemical weapons treaties, leading to a new arms race.

What might such a world look like? All major military powers could be armed with bombs, missiles, shells, and spray tanks on unmanned aerial drones, loaded with chemical agents that cause stupor, convulsions, panic attacks, hallucinations, or violent sensory experiences; or with genetically engineered biological agents that degrade paint, plastic, rubber, fuel, and lubricants. Some regional powers would have stockpiles of lethal agents like third-generation nerve gases and genetically engineered pathogens. Non-lethal chemical weapons, anti-materiel weapons, and possibly also lethal chemical and biological weapons would likely be used repeatedly in regional conflicts. The proliferation of these technologies would dramatically increase the chances that terrorists would become capable of mass-casualty attacks using chemical or bioweapons. Police forces would be armed with new riot control agents, based on military non-lethal weapons that are much more effective than tear gas. This would greatly increase government power to control civil unrest—a dangerous tool in totalitarian hands, and one for which democracies have little use.

Technological Superiority in Weaponry

For decades, the United States has based its military strategy on maintaining technological superiority. A program that includes exploring new ways to make weapons using biotech would be an appealing response to the threat of bioweapons. But besides helping the military understand that threat, such a program would also constitute a first step toward an offensive capability.

The United States appears to have embarked on a largely classified study . . . of biotech applications for the development of new bioweapons.

Of great concern are the calls from the U.S. military to alter or eliminate the bioweapons treaty. Doing so would allow it to develop genetically engineered bioweapons that target military materiel like camouflage paint, tires, stealth coatings, electronic insulation, runway tarmac, lubricants, and fuel.

For more than a decade the military has been exploiting a loophole in the Chemical Weapons Convention that permits chemical agents for law enforcement purposes. It has actively pursued development of non-lethal chemical weapons with the expectation of someday using them in military operations other than war (counterterrorism, hostage rescue, embassy protection, peacekeeping operations, etc.).

The United States is also developing munitions to deliver its non-lethal chemical agents. More and more, biotechnology is being used for this program. Reproducing this approach in its biodefense program would be a natural step for the military. Indeed, the same agency that administers the non-lethal chemical weapons program has serious interest in—and apparently projects on—genetically engineered non-lethal bioweapons. This is pioneering very dangerous ground.

Sparking a Global Bioweapons Arms Race

The United States appears to have embarked on a largely classified study, across several agencies, of biotech applications for the development of new bioweapons. The clandestine U.S. programs indicate a willingness to ignore treaty law in favor of maintaining technological superiority in response to the emerging bioweapons threat. And U.S. behavior suggests that its biodefense program is even larger than those portions that have been revealed. This U.S. exploration of the utility of biotech for bioweapons development is unwise, for the rest of the world will be obliged to follow suit. In its rush to stay ahead technologically, the United States runs the risk of leading the world down a path toward much-reduced security. More than 30 years ago, the United States ended its offensive bioweapons program in part because it feared that the program's very existence invited other nations to imitate it. That wisdom seems to have been forgotten.

Once bioweapons are established in military arsenals and in planning, they will be considered legitimate.

Furthermore, the secrecy required by such a program is antithetical to the transparency on which long-term bioweapons control must be founded. It could also spark a global bioweapons arms race. A world in which many nations are secretly exploring the offensive military applications of biotech would be ripe for proliferation. If a country doesn't know its enemy's offensive capabilities, military strategists must assume the worst—that the enemy possesses or is developing bioweapons. This will provoke the development of bioweapons for a retaliatory or deterrent capability. And once bioweapons are established in military arsenals and in planning, they will be considered legitimate.

187

Organizations to Contact

The Acronym Institute for Disarmament Diplomacy
24 Colvestone Crescent, London   E8 2LH
   United Kingdom
(44) 207-503-8857
e-mail: rej@acronym.org.uk
Web site: www.acronym.org.uk

The Acronym Institute works to promote effective approaches to international security, disarmament, and arms control. It provides reporting, analysis, and strategic thinking on these issues, with special emphasis on treaties and multilateral initiatives. It publishes the journal *Disarmament Diplomacy* six times a year as well as reports and statements on weapons issues. Its Web site database contains a listing of all known global WMD possessors.

The American Association for
the Advancement of Science (AAAS)
1200 New York Ave. NW, 11th Floor, Washington, DC   20005
(202) 326-6493 • fax: (202) 289-4958
e-mail: jciambor@aaas.org
Web site: www.aaas.org

AAAS is an international nonprofit organization dedicated to advancing science and serving society. It publishes the peer-reviewed journal *Science* and sponsors the Center for Science, Technology, and Security Policy. The center seeks to advise policy makers by providing the best scientific facts and thinking on security issues. The AAAS Web site contains articles on science and WMD, including "Bioterrorism in a Threatening World."

American Enterprise Institute (AEI)
1150 Seventeenth St. NW, Washington, DC   20036
(202) 862-5800 • fax: (202) 862-7177
e-mail: info@aei.org
Web site: www.aei.org

Formally known as The American Enterprise Institute for Public Policy Research, AEI is a scholarly research institute that is dedicated to preserving a strong foreign policy and national defense. It publishes the magazine *American Enterprise* and promotes forums on current national defense and foreign policy issues. The institute's Web site has a large section of archived and current articles by institute scholars on weapons of mass destruction.

Arms Control Association (ACA)
1726 M St. NW, Suite 201, Washington, DC   20036
(202) 463-8270 • fax: (202) 463-8273
e-mail: aca@armscontrol.org
Web site: www.armscontrol.org

The Arms Control Association is a nonprofit organization dedicated to promoting public understanding and support of effective arms control policies. ACA seeks to increase public appreciation of the need to limit arms, reduce international tensions, and promote peaceful solutions to global conflict. It publishes the monthly magazine *Arms Control Today*.

Brookings Institution
1775 Massachusetts Ave. NW, Washington, DC   20036
(202) 797-6000 • fax: (202) 797-6004
e-mail: brookinfo@brook.edu
Web site: www.brookings.org

The Brookings Institution is a think tank that conducts research on foreign policy, economics, government, and the social sciences. The Saban Center for Middle East Policy at the Brookings Institution develops programs to educate the public on policy choices made in the Middle East. It publishes the quarterly *Brookings Review* among other publications.

Carnegie Endowment for International Peace
1779 Massachusetts Ave. NW, Washington, DC   20036
(202) 483-7600 • fax: (202) 483-1840
e-mail: info@ceip.org
Web site: www.ceip.org

The Carnegie Endowment researches and publishes articles on American foreign policy and international relations, focusing on strategies to reduce global tensions. Its quarterly journal *Foreign Policy* contains numerous articles by Carnegie Endowment fellows regarding nuclear weapons and proliferation.

Cato Institute
1000 Massachusetts Ave. NW, Washington, DC   20001-5403
(202) 842-0200 • fax: (202) 842-3490
e-mail: cato@cato.org
Web site: www.cato.org

The Cato Institute is a libertarian public policy research foundation dedicated to limiting the role of government and promoting free markets based on international peace. The institute does not support an interventionist foreign policy and believes that the use of U.S. forces in foreign countries should be limited. It publishes the quarterly magazine *Regulation*, the bimonthly *Cato Policy Report*, and numerous position papers dealing with foreign policy.

Center for Defense Information (CDI)
1779 Massachusetts Ave. NW, Suite 615
  Washington, DC   20036
(202) 332-0600 • fax: (202) 462-4559
e-mail: info@cdi.org
Web site: www.cdi.org

CDI is composed of civilian weapons experts and former military officers who oppose an overfunded Pentagon weapons budget and policies that promote conflict and war. Its watchdog publication *Defense Monitor*, published ten times a year, analyzes military weapons spending, policies, and systems.

Center for Nonproliferation Studies
Monterey Institute for International Studies
  Monterey, CA   93940
(831) 647-4154 • fax: (831)-647-3519
Web site: http://cns.miis.edu

The center researches all aspects of nonproliferation and works to combat the spread of weapons of mass destruction. The center produces research databases and publishes reports, papers, speeches, and congressional testimony online. The center's main publication is the *Nonproliferation Review*, which is published three times a year.

Center for Strategic and International Studies (CSIS)
1800 K St. NW, Suite 400, Washington, DC   20006
(202) 884-0200 • fax: (202) 775-3199
Web site: www.csis.org

CSIS aims to provide world leaders with strategic analyses and policy options on current and emerging global issues. It publishes books and the *Washington Quarterly*, a forum for political, economic, and security-related issues.

Chemical and Biological Arms Control Institute
2111 Eisenhower Ave., Suite 302, Alexandria, VA   22314
(703) 739-1538 • fax: (703) 739-1525
e-mail: cbaci@cbaci.org
Web site: www.cbaci.org

The institute is a nonprofit corporation that supports arms control and nonproliferation, specializing in chemical and biological weapons. The institute seeks to influence weapons-control treaties through seminars and numerous monographs, fact sheets, and reports. Its main print publication is the *Dispatch*, which is produced bimonthly.

Council on Foreign Relations
58 E. Sixty-eighth St., New York, NY   10021
(212) 434-9400 • fax: (212) 986-2984
e-mail: communications@cfr.org
Web site: www.cfr.org

The council specializes in foreign affairs and studies the international aspects of American political and economic policies and problems. It publishes the journal *Foreign Affairs* five times a year, which includes articles by foreign policy experts analyzing America's political, economic, and military relations with the global community.

Henry L. Stimson Center
11 Dupont Circle NW, 9th Floor, Washington, DC   20036
(202) 223-5956 • fax: (202) 238-9604
Web site: www.stimson.org

The Stimson Center in an independent nonprofit public policy institute committed to crafting solutions to U.S. and foreign security challenges. The center directs the Chemical and Biological Weapons Nonproliferation Project, a data resource related to monitoring and implementation of the 1993 Chemical Weapons Convention. The center produces occasional papers, reports, fact sheets, and books related to policies for eradicating WMD.

The Heritage Foundation
214 Massachusetts Ave. NE, Washington, DC   20002
(202) 546-4400 • fax: (202) 546-8328
e-mail: info@heritage.org
Web site: www.heritage.org

The Heritage Foundation is a conservative public policy research institute. It holds seminars and forums and publishes position papers and research reports on topics deemed vital to America's security and interests. Its Web site contains articles on WMD, including speeches at foundation seminars by government officials.

Hoover Institution
Stanford University, Stanford, CA   94305-6010
(650) 723-1754 • fax: (650) 723-1687
e-mail: horaney@hoover.stanford.edu
Web site: www.hoover.stanford.edu

The Hoover Institution is a public policy research center devoted to advanced study and scholarship in politics, economics, and international affairs. It publishes the quarterly *Hoover Digest* and *Policy Review*, which include articles on WMD and America's foreign policy. The institute also publishes special reports and a newsletter.

Institute for Defense and Disarmament Studies
675 Massachusetts Ave., 8th Floor, Cambridge, MA   02139
(617) 354-4337 • fax: (617) 354-1450
Web site: www.idds.org

IDDS is a nonprofit center dedicated to the study of global military policies, arms holdings, production and trade, arms control, and peace-building efforts. It publishes the journals *ArmsWatch 2005, Arms Control Reporter,* and *World Arms Database.* Its Web site contains numerous articles on WMD-related topics.

Middle East Forum
1500 Walnut St., Suite 1050, Philadelphia, PA   19102
(215) 546-5406 • fax: (215) 546-5409
e-mail: info@meforum.org
Web site: www.meforum.org

The Middle East Forum is a think tank that works to define and promote American interests in the Middle East. It supports strong American ties with Israel, Turkey, and other democracies. It publishes the *Middle East Quarterly,* a policy-oriented journal. Its Web site includes articles, summaries of activities, and a discussion forum.

Middle East Institute

1761 N St. NW, Washington, DC   20036-2882
(202) 785-1141 • fax: (202) 331-8861
e-mail: mideasti@mideasti.org
Web site: www.themiddleeastinstitute.org

The institute's charter mission is to promote better understanding of Middle Eastern cultures, languages, religions, and
politics. It publishes books, research papers, audiotapes, and
videos as well as the quarterly *Middle East Journal*. It also
maintains an Educational Outreach Department to supply
teachers and students of all grade levels advice on resources.

Middle East Media Research Institute (MEMRI)

PO Box 27837, Washington, DC   20038-7837
(202) 955-9070 • fax: (202) 955-9077
e-mail: memri@memri.org
Web site: www.memri.org

MEMRI translates and disseminates articles and commentaries
from Middle East media sources and attempts to improve understanding between the West and the Middle East. Its Web
site provides access to dispatches from the Middle East such as
"Arab Media Reactions to Libya's Announcement of WMD
Disarmament."

Middle East Policy Council

1730 M St. NW, Suite 512, Washington, DC   20036-4505
(202) 296-6767 • fax: (202) 296-5791
e-mail: info@mepc.org
Web site: www.mepc.org

The Middle East Policy Council was founded in 1981 to expand public discussion and understanding of issues affecting
U.S. policy in the Middle East. The council is a nonprofit educational organization that operates nationwide. It publishes
the quarterly *Middle East Policy Journal*.

Project for the New American Century
1150 Seventeenth St. NW, Suite 510, Washington, DC 20036
(202) 293-4983 • fax: (202) 293-4572
e-mail: project@newamericancentury.org
Web site: www.newamericancentury.org

The Project of the New American Century is a nonprofit educational organization dedicated to the propositions that American leadership is good both for America and for the world and that such leadership requires military strength, diplomatic engagement, and commitment to moral principle. The project provides issue briefs, research papers, advocacy journalism, and seminars to define American global leadership. Its Web site includes project papers such as "Iraq: Setting the Record Straight," "Rebuilding America's Defenses," and "The No-Nukes Party."

Union of Concerned Scientists (UCS)
2 Brattle Sq., Cambridge, MA 02238
(617) 547-5552 • fax: (617) 864-9405
e-mail: ucs@ucsusa.org
Web site: www.ucsusa.org

UCS works to report on the impact of advanced technology on society. It supports nuclear arms control as a means to reduce nuclear weapons. It publishes the quarterly newsletter *Nucleus* as well as reports and news items related to nuclear proliferation.

United Nations (UN)
First Ave. at Forty-Sixth St., New York, NY 10017
Web site: www.un.org

The UN is an international organization dedicated to maintaining international peace and security, developing friendly relations among nations, and promoting international cooperation. Articles and speeches about WMD are available on its Web site.

United States Department of State
2201 C St. NW, Washington, DC   20520
(202) 647-4000
Web site: www.state.gov

The State Department is the lead agency responsible for U.S. foreign affairs. It seeks to shape a free, secure, and prosperous world by formulating, representing, and implementing the president's foreign policy. Its Web site contains speeches and position papers on WMD, including "China and Proliferation of Weapons of Mass Destruction and Missiles: Policy Issues" and "Nuclear Nonproliferation Issues."

Washington Institute for Near East Policy
1828 L St. NW, Suite 1050, Washington, DC   20036
(202) 452-0650 • fax: (202) 223-5364
e-mail: info@washingtoninstitute.org
Web site: www.washintoninstitute.org

The institute is an independent nonprofit research organization that provides information and analysis on the Middle East and U.S. policy in that region. It publishes numerous books, monographs, and reports related to regional politics, security, and economics.

Bibliography

Books

Graham Allison — *Nuclear Terrorism: The Ultimate Preventable Catastrophe.* New York: Times Books, 2004.

Berhanykun Andemicael and John Mathiason — *Eliminating Weapons of Mass Destruction: Prospects for Effective International Verification.* New York: Palgrave Macmillan, 2005.

Hans Blix — *Disarming Iraq.* New York: Pantheon, 2004.

Olivia Bosch and Peter Van Ham — *Global Non-proliferation and Counterterrorism: The Impact of UNSCR 1540.* Washington, DC: Brookings Institution, 2005.

Peter Brookes — *A Devil's Triangle: Terrorism, Weapons of Mass Destruction, and Rogue States.* Lanham, MD: Rowman & Littlefield, 2005.

Kurt M. Campbell, Robert J. Einhorn, and Mitchell B. Reiss — *The Nuclear Tipping Point: Why States Reconsider Their Nuclear Choices.* Washington, DC: Brookings Institution, 2004.

Joseph Cirincione, John B. Wolfsthal, Miriam Rajkumar — *Deadly Arsenals: Tracking Weapons of Mass Destruction.* Washington, DC: Carnegie Endowment for International Peace, 2002.

Commission on the Intelligence Capabilities of the United States Regarding Weapons of Mass Destruction	*Report to the President of the United States.* North Charleston, SC: BookSurge, 2005.
Jason D. Ellis and Geoffrey D. Kiefer	*Combating Proliferation: Strategic Intelligence and Security Policy.* Baltimore: Johns Hopkins University Press, 2004.
Charles D. Ferguson and William C. Potter	*The Four Faces of Nuclear Terrorism.* New York: Routledge, 2005.
Lyle J. Goldstein	*Preventive Attack and Weapons of Mass Destruction: A Comparative Historical Survey.* Palo Alto, CA: Stanford University Press, 2005.
Jeanne Guillemin	*Biological Weapons: From the Invention of State-Sponsored Programs to Contemporary Bioterrorism.* New York: Columbia University Press, 2004.
Nadine Gurr and Benjamin Cole	*The New Face of Terrorism: Threats from Weapons of Mass Destruction.* London: Tauris, 2002.
Robert Harris and Jeremy Paxman	*A Higher Form of Killing: The Secret History of Chemical and Biological Warfare.* New York: Random House, 2002.

Stuart E. Johnson and William H. Lewis — *Weapons of Mass Destruction: New Perspectives on Counterproliferation.* Honolulu: University Press of the Pacific, 2005.

Kyoung-Soo Kim, ed. — *North Korea's Weapons of Mass Destruction: Problems and Prospects.* Elizabeth, NJ: Hollym International, 2004.

Jeff Larsen, James Wirtz, and Eric Croddy, eds. — *Weapons of Mass Destruction: An Encyclopedia of Worldwide Policy, Technology, and History.* Santa Barbara, CA: ABC-CLIO, 2004.

Janne E. Nolan, Bernard I. Finel, and Brian D. Finlay, eds. — *Ultimate Security: Combating Weapons of Mass Destruction.* New York: Century Foundation, 2004.

Michael Richardson — *A Time Bomb for Global Trade: Maritime-Related Terrorism in an Age of Weapons of Mass Destruction.* Singapore: Institute of Southeast Asian Studies, 2004.

Scott Ritter — *Frontier Justice: Weapons of Mass Destruction and the Bushwhacking of America.* New York: Context, 2003.

James A. Russell, ed. — *Proliferation of Weapons of Mass Destruction in the Middle East: Directions and Policy Options in the New Century.* New York: Palgrave Macmillan, 2006.

Richard L. Russell — *Weapons Proliferation and War in the Greater Middle East: Strategic Contest.* New York: Routledge, 2006.

Scott D. Sagan and Kenneth N. Waltz	*The Spread of Nuclear Weapons: A Debate Renewed*, 2nd ed. New York: Norton, 2002.
Jonathan Schell	*The Unfinished Twentieth Century: The Crisis of Weapons of Mass Destruction*. New York: Verso, 2003.
Barry Schneider, ed.	*Middle East Security Issues: In the Shadow of Weapons of Mass Destruction Proliferation*. Honolulu: University Press of the Pacific, 2004.
Mark J. Valencia	*The Proliferation Security Initiative: Making Waves in Asia*. New York: Routledge, 2005.

Periodicals

M.C. Abad Jr.	"A Nuclear Weapon-Free Southeast Asia and Its Continuing Strategic Significance," *Contemporary Southeast Asia*, August 2005.
Marko Beljac	"WMD Proliferation and the Deadly Connection," *Arena Magazine*, December 2002.
Barry R. Bloom	"Bioterrorism and the University," *Harvard Magazine*, November 3, 2002.
Ashton B. Carter	"How to Counter WMD," *Foreign Affairs*, September/October 2004.
Alexander Cockburn	"Meet the Prime WMD Fabricator," *Nation*, August 2003.

Economist	"If You Push, I'll Shove; Weapons of Mass Destruction in the Middle East," July 10, 2004.
Daniel Eisenberg	"WMD Myth and Reality," *Time*, October 18, 2004.
Murhaf Jouejati	"Syrian Motives for Its WMD Programs and What to Do About Them," *Middle East Journal*, Winter 2005.
Hans M. Kristensen	"The Role of U.S. Nuclear Weapons: New Doctrine Falls Short of Bush Pledge," *Arms Control Today*, September 2005.
William Langewiesche	"The Wrath of Kahn: How A.Q. Kahn Made Pakistan a Nuclear Power—and Showed That the Spread of Atomic Weapons Can't Be Stopped," *Atlantic*, November 2005.
Juana Carrasco Martín	"WMD: Who's Got Them?" *Political Affairs*, online edition, October 4–9, 2004. www.politicalaffairs.net.
Daniel McKivergan	"The Worst of Intentions: What Saddam's Iraq Was Up To," *Daily Standard*, July 1, 2005. www.weekly standard.com.
Gregory Mone	"Iraq, Science and the Elusive WMD: Proof of a Bioterror Program Is Hard to Come By," *Popular Science*, January 1, 2004.

Robert R. Monroe "New Threats, Old Weapons," *Washington Post*, November 16, 2004. www.washingtonpost.com.

Tom Moriarity "Entering the Valley of Uncertainty: The Future of Preemptive Attack," *World Affairs*, Fall 2004.

Kurt Pitzer "The WMDs That Walked Away: How the U.S. Lost Track of Iraq's Nuclear Scientists," *Mother Jones*, September/October 2005.

Bill Powell "The End of the World: Is There Any Way to Stop the Spread of Nuclear Weapons?" *Fortune*, October 27, 2003.

Ed Regis "Our Own Anthrax: Dismantling America's Weapons of Mass Destruction," *Harper's Magazine*, July 2004.

Scott Ritter "Rude Awakening to Missile-Defense Dream," *Christian Science Monitor*, January 4, 2005. www.csmonitor.com.

Ronald Bruce St. John "Libya Is Not Iraq: Preemptive Strikes, WMD and Diplomacy," *Middle East Journal*, Summer 2004.

Richard Stone "New Initiatives Reach Out to Iraq's Scientific Elite," *Science*, March 12, 2004.

Jeremy Tamsett "The Israeli Bombing of Osiraq Reconsidered: Successful Counterproliferation?" *Nonproliferation Review*, Fall/Winter 2004.

Jake Tapper   "The Hyping of Saddam's WMD,"
                       Salon.com, June 18, 2003. www.salon
                       .com.

Jason Vest   "Big Lies, Blind Spies, and *Vanity
                       Fair*: Quick Lessons from the WMD
                       Report," *Village Voice*, April 7, 2005.

Ian Willams   "Blix Not Bombs," *Nation*, April 5,
                       2004.

Index

complexity makes use of WMDs by terrorists unlikely, 58–61

nuclear x-ray laser, 63

U.S. military strategy of superiority in, 185, 186

weapons, is part of global economy, 16

Teller, Edward, 63

Tenet, George, 27, 73, 74, 126, 132

terrorists

acquisition of WMDs by, 14, 26, 30

retaliating against, 92

technological complexity makes use of WMDs by, unlikely, 58–61

threat from, requires change in U.S. strategy, 81

use of biological weapons by, 183–84

censoring scientific information will help fight, 84–87

strong public infrastructure is best defense against, 88–91

were in Iraq under Hussein, 119

Test Bed, 71–72

Thompson, Tommy, 91

Times (London newspaper), 102–103

Timmerman, Kenneth R., 104

Tokyo (Japan), 59–60

treaties

defense, 147, 175

limiting biological weapons, 148, 179–83

limiting chemical weapons, 16

limiting missiles, 66, 70, 74, 148

limiting nuclear weapons, 16, 33, 70, 146

limiting weapons of individual destruction, 52–53

unilateral preemption. *See* preemption doctrine

unipolar world, 69

United Nations (UN)

does not enforce arms embargoes, 52

Monitoring, Verification and Inspection Commission (UNMOVIC), 154, 159

oil-for-food program, 102–103, 107

Security Council

Resolution 1441, 105

Resolution 1540, 157, 162

weapons inspectors, 22, 24, 124, 133

United States

accommodation with former Soviet Union nations, 67–69

aggression is threat to global security, 54–57

biological weapons

American program for, 183–87

defenses against
censoring scientific information, 88–91
rejecting Biological Weapons Convention protocol, 179, 181–83
strong public infrastructure, 88–91

chemical weapons program, 186

commitment to South Korea, 40–41

exports proliferation, 175, 176, 177

intelligence reports

about nuclear weapons in New York City, 27–28